D0175048

To Sell or Not To Sell… Employer Retirement Plans

THE FINANCIAL ADVISOR'S
ROADMAP TO A SUCCESSFUL
RETIREMENT PLANS PRACTICE

TOM FOSTER | TODD D. THOMPSON

KAPLAN PUBLISHING

This book is for informational purposes only. It does not provide business or legal advice, and should not be relied on as such. Neither the authors nor the publisher guarantees or warrants that the information in this book is accurate, complete, up to date, or will produce certain financial results. This information is general in nature and may not apply to particular factual or legal circumstances. Laws and procedures change from state to state and county to county and are subject to differing interpretations. This book is not intended to substitute for legal advice obtained from competent, independent legal counsel in the relevant jurisdiction. If you want legal advice, please consult a lawyer. This book is not intended to create—and your use of this book does not constitute—a business or lawyer-client relationship between you and the authors or publisher of this book. This book is not a substitute for sound business and legal judgment, and you should not act upon any of the information in this book without first confirming that the suggestions, processes, documents, and information in this book are appropriate for your situation. All real-life stories are to the best of the authors' recollections, and proper names have all been changed to protect the people involved.

President, Kaplan Publishing: Roy Lipner
Vice President and Publisher: Maureen McMahon
Acquisitions Editor: Victoria Smith
Director of Production: Daniel Frey
Production Editor: Karen Goodfriend
Typesetter: the dotted i

Views expressed by Tom Foster and Todd Thompson are their own and do not necessarily represent the views of The Hartford Financial Services Group, Inc., its affiliates and/or subsidiaries, including but not limited to the issuing companies of Hartford Life Insurance Company and Hartford Life and Annuity Insurance Company (collectively, "The Hartford"). The Hartford makes no warranty, expressed or implied, and assumes no legal liability or responsibility for the accuracy, completeness, timeliness, or usefulness of any information in this book. Without limiting the foregoing, the information in this book may not be relied upon for the purpose of avoiding IRS penalties. As with all matters of a tax or legal nature, individuals should consult their own tax or legal counsel for advice. The definition of retirement "plans" as referred to in this text means various services and processes that financial professionals provide.

© 2007 by E. Thomas Foster, Jr., Esq., and Todd D. Thompson

Published by Kaplan Publishing

All rights reserved. The text of this publication, or any part thereof, may not be reproduced in any manner whatsoever without written permission from the publisher.

Printed in the United States of America

07 08 09 10 9 8 7 6 5 4 3 2 1

Library of Congress Cataloging-in-Publication Data
Foster, E. Thomas.
    To sell or not to sell– employer retirement plans : the financial professional's road map to a successful retirement plans practice / by E. Thomas Foster and Todd D. Thompson.
        p. cm.
    ISBN-13: 978-1-4195-9325-3
    ISBN-10: 1-4195-9325-0
    1. Pension trusts–United States. I. Thompson, Todd D. II. Title.
    HD7105.45.U6F67 2007
    331.25'20688–dc22
                                    2006034503

Kaplan Publishing books are available at special quantity discounts to use for sales promotions, employee premiums, or educational purposes. Please call our Special Sales Department to order or for more information at 800-621-9621 ext. 4444, e-mail *kaplanpubsales@kaplan.com*, or write to Kaplan Publishing, 30 South Wacker Drive, Suite 2500, Chicago, IL 60606-7481.

ENDORSEMENTS

"Tom and Todd provide compelling reasons for selling employer retirement plans. Financial professionals who are already engaged in this business should greatly benefit from Tom and Todd's timely insights to the opportunities created by the recent passage of the Pension Protection Act. To Sell or Not to Sell *is a must for any financial professional who wants to get into the employer retirement plan market because it provides specific instructions about what is needed to be successful. Financial professionals who follow Tom and Todd's advice should be richly rewarded for their efforts."*

TED BENNA

President of the 401(k) Association and chief operating officer of
Malvern Benefits Corporation and a nationally recognized expert on retirement issues.
He is commonly referred to as the "father of 401(k)."

"Tom and Todd have managed to take a very complex and sometimes scary topic—the emerging intricacies and complexities of retirement plan legislation and plan design—and turn it into a powerful, proactive selling and relationship management tool for the financial professional. Through To Sell or Not to Sell, *they explain these complexities in plain English, and they make it fun! I would recommend this book as a must-read for any financial professional who wants to break into the retirement plans business."*

FRED REISH

Pension attorney with Reish Luftman Reicher & Cohen and a nationally known expert
on ERISA tax law and retirement plans legislation.

"Hats off to Tom Foster, Todd Thompson, and The Hartford's Retirement Plans Group for developing this powerful guide for financial professionals. Solutions Based Sales *is a process every financial professional should follow—it's simple yet powerful. It's no secret why these professionals have had such success in their businesses and in their lives. I encourage you to find out what can drive your success in retirement plan sales."*

HAL BECKER

Author of *Can I Have 5 Minutes of Your Time?*, *Lip Service*, and *Get What You Want!*
Nationally known speaker on sales and customer service.

"Having shared many moments with the executives at The Hartford, you can rest assured that this text will be filled with many winning ideas that will help you grow professionally. To put it in 'Vitalese,' it's going to be 'Awesome, baby,' with a capital A!"

DICK VITALE

Former basketball coach of the University of Detroit and the Detroit Pistons. Author of *Vitale: Time Out, Baby!* and *Campus Chaos: Why the Game I Love Is Breaking My Heart.* Currently ESPN's number-one color analyst and in high demand as a motivational speaker.

"With To Sell or Not to Sell, *Tom and Todd offer a complete package for financial professionals: a comprehensive business case, practical suggestions on tools and tactics, an appendix full of reference materials, and a step-by-step approach to build a successful retirement plans practice. They have combined their insights and real-world experience to create a compelling call to action for financial professionals—those who are just becoming aware of the opportunities in retirement plan sales as well as those who have been serving these programs for many years."*

NEVIN E. ADAMS, JD

A twenty-eight-year veteran of the retirement services industry, Adams is editor-in-chief of *PLANSPONSOR* magazine. A frequent speaker at industry and trade conferences, Adams has been quoted in multiple national publications, has appeared on CNN, and is a regular columnist in *On Wall Street* magazine.

I believe everyone needs three Fs to be successful in their business and personal lives: Family, Faith, and Friends. I'm often away from home weekends, nights, and whole weeks at a time. I wouldn't be able to do my job without the love and support of my wife Karen and my daughter Courtney. Thank you from the bottom of my heart for standing by me all these years. I love you both.

I would also like to thank my beloved parents Mary and Dr. Edwin T. Foster, my little sister Mary Jo, and my mother-in-law and father-in-law, Pauline and Arthur Jodoin. I dedicate this book to all of you. And I'd like to include another family member: my loyal, trusted little buddy for 16 years, Magnolia.

I also dedicate this book to everyone whose lives have touched me over my 32-year career—within and outside of the financial services industry. You allowed me to be me, and you all are my inspiration. One special person stands out: my uncle, Larry Sullivan, a true inspiration, who introduced me to the pension business. Thank you all.

—Tom Foster

I dedicate this book to my wife Nicole and my children, Aaron and Ashley. I know you often shook your heads at my early-morning and late-evening hours. Thank you for your gift of time so this project could reach completion.

I also dedicate this book to my mother and father, Dale and Norma Thompson, my grandparents, Bernie and Evelyn Thompson, my sister Michelle and her husband Mike Costello, The Greatos, my uncles (Bruce, Terry, and Bernie), my Aunt Linda, my ski buds (Rocket, Skippy, Bill, Doc, TA, and Bad Brad), and all my other friends and family, many of whom encouraged me to pursue the dream of sharing the information in this book and who have made me a better person.

—Todd Thompson

PART A

WHY THERE HAS NEVER BEEN A BETTER TIME TO BE IN THIS BUSINESS

PART B

SOLUTIONS BASED SELLING: THE ROAD TO A SUCCESSFUL PRACTICE

PART D

WALK A MILE IN FRANK'S SHOES

First and foremost, we wish to thank David Levenson and Jim Davey for having the vision to make this dream a reality. And we thank Amy Naeser, who was instrumental in spearheading this project. We are especially grateful and indebted to our quarterback, Tim Benedict. Tim's leadership, focus, and vision have been stellar.

Special thanks to these gentlemen for their support of this project: Ramani Ayer, chairman and CEO, The Hartford Financial Services Group; Tom Marra, president and CEO, Hartford Life; and John Walters, president, U.S. Wealth Management Group, Hartford Life.

This book would never have been possible without the hard work of our editors Barbara McNichol and Patrice Rhoades-Baum. They did a phenomenal job and we truly appreciate their help. We also wish to acknowledge Victoria Smith and the entire production team at Kaplan Publishing.

A personal note from Tom Foster:
I would like to thank all my friends at The Hartford for giving me the honor and privilege of being their national retirement plans spokesperson. I would like to give a special thanks to my phenomenal assistant Mary Sawicki—I couldn't do my job without her.

I would also like to acknowledge all the nuns, priests, professors, and friends at Our Lady of Sacred Heart School, Cathedral High School, American International College, Holy Cross College, and Suffolk Law School.

The inspiration for this project came from my close friend and colleague Todd Thompson: the consummate salesperson, professional, and friend. And so, Todd, a special thanks from your friend forever.

A personal note from Todd Thompson:
I would like to thank Tom Foster, his wife, and his daughter for being great friends. Tom's efforts helped take this book from a stack of papers sitting in my office to a published book.

I would also like to acknowledge Derek Fuller and Kevin Kirk for giving me a chance six years ago, and for their leadership and patience while this book was developed. Thanks, too, to Dr. Jones, Ron Hill, Bob Fairclough, Thomas Stuker, the authors of the helpful books I have read, and everyone who has helped to shape me into a successful person.

THE TIME IS RIGHT—DON'T SHY AWAY FROM THIS OPPORTUNITY TO GROW YOUR BUSINESS

Several years ago, we noticed a big difference between financial professionals who consistently sell employer-sponsored retirement plans and those who either don't sell retirement plans or sell only a handful a year. Today, only a small percentage of financial professionals actively sell retirement plans but across the board, their income levels prove they're doing so successfully. Meanwhile, the majority of financial professionals miss out on a fabulous opportunity.

What's the opportunity?

Two major factors are at play here:

1. Businesses with fewer than 1,000 employees have a tremendous need to provide incentives for their employees.
2. Vast numbers of employees in the United States (particularly baby boomers between age 45 and 60) require opportunities and vehicles to save for their retirement *today*.

In short, the time is right to be in this business.

So why are only a few financial professionals successfully selling retirement plans? In a word: *misconceptions*. They believe too many salespeople are already out there and the competition is intense.

Often, when presenting to a group of financial professionals, we ask these questions:

- "Do you sell mutual funds? If so, please raise your hands." Every person's hand shoots into the air.

- "Do you sell annuities?" Nearly everyone's hand remains in the air.
- "Do you sell employer-sponsored retirement plans?" Most hands drop; only a few remain up.

Then these professionals look around the room. When they see this response, it rocks their belief that the retirement plans niche is too competitive. In reality, if you enter this business, you're only competing against a small number of other financial professionals.

That's one misconception about this business. We've discovered a lot more—misconceptions that discourage financial professionals from getting their feet wet in the retirement plans market. So we're here to set the record straight. We're here to encourage financial professionals like you to seriously consider entering this niche and growing your practice.

This book is our vehicle. Within these pages, we'll give you step-by-step guidance to get started and be successful in the retirement plans business. We'll start by revealing the three critical secrets of those top producers who are building lucrative practices through employer-sponsored retirement plans sales.

SECRET 1: BUILD RELATIONSHIPS, TRUST, AND CONFIDENCE

Too many people pitch "product," either a single product or a spreadsheet of several products. But the retirement plans business isn't about *product*. It's about building relationships so you can earn your prospect's or client's trust and confidence. Using this sales approach can significantly increase your closing ratio, which, of course, positively affects your business and income. Chapter 5 is dedicated to teaching you how to build relationships using Solutions Based Selling.

Todd's Story: Building Relationships, Trust, and Confidence Leads to Sales—No Matter What Business You're In

On a recent trip to the mountain states with one of my salespeople, we happened into a tiny town called Ennis, the fly-fishing capital of Montana. I've been fly-fishing a few times, but I'm from Wisconsin so I wasn't familiar with the tackle needs for the cold, rushing waters of Montana. I needed to buy tackle, but mostly I needed information about fishing in this area.

The town of Ennis sports two fly-fishing shops. I stopped in the first shop and asked the salesperson what kind of tackle I'd need for fly-fishing locally. He rattled off umpteen items and tossed in, "Don't forget to get tippets and indicators."

"What are *tippets* and *indicators?*" I wondered.

I didn't ask. I didn't want to look foolish. I walked around the shop looking for anything labeled *tippet* or *indicator.* Nothing. I left empty-handed and somewhat embarrassed.

Then I walked down the street to the second shop, approached the salesperson there, and asked him the same question. "Do you have a few minutes to answer some questions?" he replied. He then engaged me in multiple questions including these: "How many times have you been fly-fishing? Did you go with or without a guide? Where did you go? What kind of fish were you after? What kind of tackle did you use? For this trip, do you want the services of a guide?"

We talked for more than 20 minutes. In fact, our conversation meandered way off fishing! At the end of our discussion, he showed me exactly what I needed to buy, including tippets and indicators. (It turns out that a tippet refers to fishing line, and an indicator is simply Montana's word for bobber, which attaches to the fishing line and bobs in the water to indicate where the line is.)

If Jeff, this charismatic and helpful salesperson, had told me I needed to fish with a net and use live bait, I would have bought a net and used live bait—that's how credible he was. Jeff had taken the time to get to know me and had earned my trust and confidence. With mastery, he helped me make good buying decisions to meet my fly-fishing needs that day.

If I hadn't spent time with Jeff, I might have bought a few flies, gone fishing somewhere, and maybe caught a few fish if I was lucky. But Jeff helped me do it right—to select the right tackle and hire the right guide. Sure enough, we caught a lot of fish that day. If I ever return to Ennis, even if I'm just passing through, I'll stop in that tackle shop just to say hello to Jeff. In fact, I plan to send him a thank-you gift.

I started as an uneducated buyer; Jeff's knowledge and guidance helped me become a more confident and successful angler.

The bottom line: Salespeople who gain their clients' trust build positive, long-term relationships.

SECRET 2: TOP PRODUCERS SHARE COMMON CHARACTERISTICS

Financial professionals who consistently sell employer-sponsored retirement plans share these traits: determination, commitment, and perseverance. These businesspeople don't lose faith if they don't win a sale. They simply don't give up. In fact, much like a Major League Baseball player, when they get one hit out of every three times at bat, they're considered among the best players.

What other traits do these top producers share? Consider these:

- Top performers understand the importance of client retention and how this dramatically affects their ancillary business opportunities. (In Chapter 2, you'll find impressive revenue numbers that translate into compelling reasons to get into this business and *stay* in it.)
- They have a common approach to the business. They adopt a structured approach for each sale and use a structured formula for success. (You'll learn about this approach throughout this book.)
- They're committed to *working with experts* instead of *trying to be the expert*. (You'll learn how to build your team of experts in Chapter 7.)
- Finally, they're passionate about the retirement plans business because they learn about the sales process, take time to

understand the viewpoints of plan sponsors (employers), know how to present solutions to meet employers' needs, and clearly understand the ancillary opportunities this business offers.

SECRET 3: TOP PRODUCERS UNDERSTAND HOW TO CLOSE; THEY ASK FOR THE BUSINESS

For the retirement plans industry, top-performing financial professionals may typically close 30 to 40 percent of their sales opportunities. Just like Major League Baseball hitters, this is a terrific statistic. Do these top producers work long hours preparing more on proposals than usual? *No.* Do they beat out their competitors by quoting low prices? *No.* Do they do their research, build solid relationships with their clients, present solutions (not products) to their clients, and then ask for the sale? *Yes.*

Surprisingly, asking for the sale is the "trick up their sleeve" that their competitors often miss. One of our top performers at The Hartford, a retirement plans specialist we'll call Michael, consistently closes 65 percent of his proposals. That's two hits out of every three times at bat!

When he came on board with The Hartford in 2004, Michael was taught the Solutions Based Selling approach. This approach emphasizes the solutions presented to clients to meet their needs and solve their problems rather than emphasizing selling a product. It instills trust and confidence as you build relationships with your clients. (Be patient. You'll learn step by step how to implement this approach by following the action points in this book.)

As it turns out, Michael is naturally a huge "relationship" guy. Throughout the sales process, he creates amazing relationships with financial professionals and plan sponsors. His success directly results from building a relationship with each of these individuals.

Interestingly, when The Hartford recruited Michael, he wasn't sure he would be successful at selling employer-sponsored retirement plans. In fact, it took a convincing sales job to get him on board because he had many objections—probably the same ones you have. But today, there's no stopping him. We first showed Michael the great opportunities that lie ahead and then convinced him to get into this business. (When we get together today, we joke about how we needed to convince him then.)

We're certain that you can have similar success after reading this book. You'll learn first, *why* you need to be in this business and second, *how* you can be successful at it. Read on and step into your future.

E. Thomas Foster, Jr., Esq.
National Spokesperson for The Hartford's Employer Retirement Plans

Todd D. Thompson
Vice President, North Central Division, for The Hartford's Retirement Plans Group

WHY THERE HAS NEVER BEEN A BETTER TIME TO BE IN THIS BUSINESS

1

A GROWING
(AND EVOLVING) MARKET

*"Every day you empower yourself to become a little bit better
or a little bit worse."*

–Jim Flanigan

"There has never been a better
time in history to sell retirement plans!"

Although we've been making this statement for almost a decade,
the opportunities afforded by providing employer-sponsored retirement plans are multiplying rapidly today. Specifically, we're referring
to retirement plans that employers sponsor and offer to their employees. The employer may be a large, public corporation; a privately
owned small- to mid-size business; a nonprofit organization (such as
a regional charity); or a tax-exempt governmental group (such as a
school system).

Let's look at what has brought retirement plans to this point in
history and see why this incredible opportunity can be great for you,
the financial professional, as the next step to profitably expanding
your business.

Above all, the employer-sponsored retirement plans market has
been one of frequent change and complexity since our friend ERISA
(defined below) first arrived on the scene about three decades ago.
Yet within the change and complexity that ERISA brings to your pro-

fession are enterprising opportunities for you. You *can* capture an increasingly profitable piece of a rapidly growing market.

THE EVOLVING REGULATORY LANDSCAPE OF ERISA

As a financial professional, you may know much of the ERISA story that follows. As you read, keep in mind how laws and regulations tended to create the foundation for employer-sponsored retirement plans—and the inherent opportunities that this market offers.

Just a few decades ago, the 401(k), now a household word across the United States, was simply a tax code and letters. The Employee Retirement Income Security Act of 1974 (ERISA) changed the retirement landscape forever in this country when it revolutionized the employer-sponsored retirement market. ERISA cleared the path for the introduction of the 401(k) in 1978.

Simply stated, ERISA is a federal law that sets minimum standards for pension plans in private industry. For example, businesses offering retirement plans must regularly provide participants with information about plan features and funding. In addition, ERISA:

- Sets minimum standards for participation, vesting, benefit accrual, and funding
- Requires accountability of plan fiduciaries (company directors or other principals)
- Gives participants the right to sue for benefits and breaches of fiduciary duty
- Guarantees payment of certain benefits through the Pension Benefit Guaranty Corporation (a federally chartered corporation) if a defined benefit plan is terminated

Title 1 of ERISA gave the Department of Labor's Employee Benefits Security Administration the authority to set regulations and enforce ERISA laws. Title 2 empowered the U.S. Treasury to interpret the ERISA law for taxation purposes. Sounds simple, right? Wrong. This is where the complexity really begins.

Pension Protection Act of 2006 Offers Positive Changes and Creates Opportunities for Financial Professionals

We're excited about the Pension Protection Act of 2006 ("the Act"), newly passed legislation that provides layers of opportunities over the next several years.

The Act's multiple measures offer terrific opportunities for financial professionals to educate employers and employees on positive changes that can impact their retirement plans. Plus, many provisions don't kick in until 2007 and beyond. The Act's staggered effective dates create multiple opportunities to be proactive and educate clients about how the new measures affect them. We see the Pension Protection Act of 2006 as a great way to attract new prospects and reinforce client retention.

Here are some of the changes you can discuss with your clients, along with their effective dates.

Economic Growth and Tax Relief Reconciliation Act of 2001 (EGTRRA) permanency. One provision in the Pension Protection Act of 2006 makes permanent the 2001 Tax Act, formerly set to expire in 2010. If this measure had not passed, many critical benefits—such as the Roth 401(k) and higher contribution limits for 401(k)s and IRAs—would have gone by the wayside or would have reverted back to old limits. Permanency of EGTRRA is great news for financial professionals.

Nonspousal rollover. Previously, when a person died only the spouse could roll over the deceased person's retirement plan assets. Effective in 2007, the nonspousal rollover provision will apply to any beneficiary such as a child, parent, or others. This is great news from a financial planning standpoint.

Rollover of after-tax contributions expanded. This new provision, effective immediately, offers flexibility in portability. Now, with proper recordkeeping, financial professionals can help their clients roll over after-tax contributions from one qualified plan to another. This provision gives financial professionals more opportunities to determine solutions that best fit their clients' needs.

Direct deposit of tax refunds into an IRA. Effective in 2007, the Pension Protection Act provides a creative way to help people save for retirement; your clients can deposit their tax refunds *directly* into their retirement vehicles.

Tax-free withdrawals from IRAs. Previously, if a client withdrew money from an IRA and gave that amount directly to a charitable organization, they would have to pay taxes on that amount. For a limited time—2006 and 2007—Congress is allowing philanthropists who are at least 70½ years old to withdraw up to $100,000 from their IRAs and give that amount to charitable organizations without paying taxes on that money. This is a narrow window of opportunity for financial professionals who specialize in estate planning. It's also a wonderful illustration of why it's good to stay on top of changing of laws and provisions, their effective dates, and their ending dates.

Accelerated vesting. Effective in 2007, this provision affects employers' vesting schedules for 401(k) and profit-sharing plans. All contributions will be accelerated to allow employees to be fully vested and access their money sooner. Financial professionals must bring this provision to the attention of both employers and employees.

Investment guidance. Many financial professionals have been concerned about giving clients specific investment advice for their 401(k) plans because of ERISA restrictions. As the "fiduciary advisor," how does the financial professional limit liability when giving guidance? A new provision in the Pension Protection Act of 2006 gives guidelines for financial professionals to follow to reduce their exposure. Financial professionals should read these guidelines and carefully follow them to be exempt from the prohibited transaction rule.

Bankrupt plans. Let's say your client worked for ABC Company, which went bankrupt. Your client participated in the company's 401(k), and more than 50 percent of the employer-matched funds had been paid in stock. However, because ABC Company went bankrupt, the stock has no value, unfortunately impacting your client's 401(k) plan. The Pension Protection Act of 2006 allows your client to make a contribution to an

IRA that is three times the normal IRA contribution limit to help offset the deficiency of the 401(k) plan. Note that this provision is only available in 2007, 2008, and 2009.

Direct rollover to Roth IRA. Previously, to roll over a 401(k) plan to a Roth IRA required first rolling the monies into a traditional IRA, converting that to a Roth IRA, and then paying taxes on that money. Effective in 2008, the intermediate plan (the traditional IRA) will no longer be needed, making the rollover process simpler.

Automatic enrollment safe harbor. For employer-sponsored retirement plans, a direct correlation exists between employee participation and the maximum amount highly compensated employees can defer. Therefore, a low participation rate negatively affects how much company officers and other highly paid employees can defer. Effective in 2008, this provision will allow employers to enroll employees automatically into their employer-sponsored retirement plans. (Employees may opt out of the plan.) This measure helps increase savings for many workers. Plus, the increased participation enables highly compensated employees to defer more money. As long as the company strictly follows the provision's guidelines, it will meet the discrimination test. This provision creates an excellent win-win situation for the company and all employees.

401(k)/defined benefits combined plan. Today's retirees have no guaranteed income stream upon retirement. With this provision, Congress is encouraging the design of a combination of a salary deferral and defined benefits plan with the goal of giving retirees the ability to defer, gain flexibility, and have a guaranteed income stream. This provision doesn't become effective until 2010, giving the U.S. Treasury and Department of Labor time to determine how to implement and regulate this plan.

The bottom line: The Pension Protection Act of 2006 offers multiple opportunities for professionals to contact and educate prospective clients. Plus, the staggered implementation of the measures provides opportunities to offer a stair-step approach to support and educate current clients. These ongoing services will serve to cement your relationships with existing clients and new employers, too.

COMPLEXITY AND CONFUSION LEAD TO OPPORTUNITY

The retirement plans field is constantly in flux. Its changing policies, regulations, and myriad products provide fodder for confusion. However, the other side of this coin is opportunity. Wherever you find confusion, you find opportunity to do what you do best: give professional guidance to clients affected by these changes.

Let's consider two examples of why the retirement plans market is confusing for employers who consider offering a plan to their employees. The first example illustrates the potential confusion that can be created when both the Department of Labor and the U.S. Treasury interpret a law that is written by Congress. The statutory requirement from Congress stipulating that minimum distributions from qualified retirement plans must begin at age 70½ is approximately two paragraphs. The U.S. Treasury interpretation of that requirement is approximately 450 pages for three separate regulations. Imagine—it takes 450 pages to interpret a law stated in two paragraphs!

The second example illustrates the potential confusion created when a new law is passed by Congress but portions of it may not become effective for years. For example, the Economic Growth and Tax Relief Reconciliation Act (EGTRRA), passed in 2001, created the Roth 401(k). Although passed in 2001, this feature just became effective in 2006. You can see the potential for confusion created in this environment of constantly evolving federal tax laws.

But don't let this history deter you! Rather, focus on how it parlays into opportunities for education and sales, thanks to the extraordinary growth in the retirement plans market that ERISA has spawned.

PROOF OF A RAPIDLY GROWING MARKET

Unlike products that can fall in and out of favor depending on market conditions, people will always need to save for retirement.

This is true whether the nation is experiencing a bull, bear, or flat market.

No doubt about it, the market for employer-sponsored retirement plans in the United States is growing rapidly. Keep in mind that opportunities to grow your business come in two forms:

1. Winning "takeover" plans, in which companies switch plans or providers
2. Winning "start-up" plans, in which you set up new plans with companies that previously didn't have them

Both takeover and start-up plans represent significant opportunities for financial professionals in these ways:

- Existing plans tend to come up for review frequently, offering opportunities for you to meet with employers who are knowledgeable and will seriously consider your solutions.
- Takeover plans are already funded with a balance (your commission would be higher than for a new plan) and already have participating employees (the balance is virtually guaranteed to grow).
- In contrast, start-up plans offer excellent opportunities to reach business owners and employees who may not have existing relationships with any other financial professionals. Gain their trust, and these owners and employees will look to you for guidance and expertise for their myriad other investment needs.

A September 2005 report from Cerulli Associates, a research and consulting firm specializing in the financial services industry, attests to the rapid growth of the company-sponsored retirement plans market. Its findings are summarized here:

- 401(k) contributions are estimated to increase to over $300 billion each year over the next five years.

- 401(k) assets are projected to increase from more than $900 billion in 2005 to close to $3 trillion in 2010.
- This market is tremendously large—more than 56 million American workers were covered by 401(k) plans in 2006, and contributions are expected to exceed $293 billion.

Even fairly small businesses represent opportunity and profitability. The Society of Professional Asset-Managers and Record Keepers (SPARK) estimated in its 2006 marketplace update that there would be more than $42 billion in takeover assets among plans with under $10 million in assets. In addition, the report projected 15,000 to 18,000 start-up plans for the year. SPARK estimated that total takeover business in 2006 would exceed $158 billion from more than 36,000 plans changing providers.

Also, consider this 2005 statistic from the U.S. Department of Labor: Out of 38,000 retirement plans with fewer than 1,000 participants, approximately 12,000 were start-up plans, and more than 26,000 were takeover plans. Compare this with only 400 takeover plans and 200 new plans for retirement plans with more than 1,000 participants. As you can see, the market segment of small- to mid-size companies is experiencing explosive growth.

WHAT EXPLAINS THIS EXPLOSIVE GROWTH?

The reasons for this growth are numerous, but the four listed here cover the major factors affecting this market today.

1. People will always need to save for retirement.

2. The retirement funding crisis is real. According to the U.S. Census Bureau, approximately 46 million baby boomers are expected to enter the 55 to 64 age bracket between 2006 and 2020. Many of these boomers haven't saved adequately for retirement and are pressuring their employers to offer retirement plans. With the right plan, employees who are over age 50 can make additional "catch-up" contributions.

3. The number of small businesses is growing at an astonishing rate. Small businesses represent more than 99 percent of employers and employ 52 percent of the private-sector workers. Historical trends point to an ever-growing number of small business owners in the United States who are driving economic growth. According to the Tax Foundation, from 1980 to 2000:

- The number of sole proprietorships doubled, from 8.9 million to 17.9 million.
- Partnerships grew 49 percent, from 1.38 million to 2.06 million.
- S corporations grew from 545,389 to 2.86 million—an astounding 424 percent.

4. Employees are realizing they must rely on self-directed retirement plans rather than company pension plans and/or Social Security. Also called "defined benefit plans," pensions are created when employers make contributions toward their employees' retirement. From those contributions, employers pay out pensions in the form of monthly checks after their employees retire. However, such corporate pension plans are going by the wayside. And with the viability of Social Security funds in jeopardy, many workers fear that this entitlement program simply won't support them in their retirement years.

In fact, self-directed retirement plans such as 401(k)s will continue to eclipse guaranteed company pension plans and Social Security as the primary source of Americans' retirement income. According to the U.S. Social Security Administration, in 2004 Social Security accounted for only 39 percent of the income of people age 65 and older. And, in the years to come, government-sponsored plans and other guaranteed pension plans are expected to continue to play an increasingly smaller role in Americans' retirement funding sources. Given these trends, consider the large number of retirement-focused individuals that financial professionals can potentially benefit by providing employer-sponsored retirement plans. You too can tap into the small- to mid-size segment of this market (where The Hartford primarily operates)—the lion's share of this market opportunity.

Think about all the small businesses in your area. Add up the number of employees who don't have the benefit of participating in retirement vehicles that help them save their earnings on a tax-deferred basis. Then ask these all-important questions:

- How many of *your* clients are small- to mid-size business owners with fewer than 1,000 employees?
- How could these owners benefit from offering retirement plans to their employees, as some already are?
- Can you afford to ignore this solid opportunity to diversify your practice and increase your profitability?

MAKING THE MOST OF THIS GROWTH OPPORTUNITY

We've noted that complexity and change combined with rapid growth set up the perfect environment for an enterprising retirement plans practice. Employers struggling to make sense of a changing financial environment would welcome working with someone who's ready to deal with the complexities. Why not you— someone who's already in tune with providing solutions to their problems?

If you're still questioning the growth possibilities, persuasive statistics emerged from a survey conducted by *PLANSPONSOR Magazine* and The Hartford's Retirement Plans Group in 2005 (see Figure 2.1 in Chapter 2). Its results show that:

- Ten percent of the survey respondents currently sell 401(k) plans.
- Fewer than 1 percent are focusing on selling retirement plans.
- Fewer than 3 percent offer at least five plan options.

Five Compelling Reasons Why Small- to Mid-Size Businesses Need Retirement Plans

Look at the issue from your clients' point of view. They can be persuaded to explore offering retirement plans to their employees for five reasons:

1. *Promote retirement savings.* Employer-sponsored retirement plans promote retirement savings for both business owners and their employees. Experts estimate that individuals will need as much as 70 to 90 percent of their preretirement income to maintain their current lifestyle during retirement. Starting to save through an employer plan will help your clients and their employees achieve this goal.
2. *Business tax deduction.* A tax deduction is generally available to businesses that contribute to an employees' retirement plan.
3. *Reduce participants' taxes.* By establishing a retirement plan that allows pretax salary reduction contributions, those employees who participate will reduce the amount of their taxable income.
4. *Build savings.* Contributions to a qualified retirement plan and earnings can accumulate on a tax-deferred basis.
5. *Attractive employee benefit.* Businesses that provide a retirement plan more easily attract and retain good employees.

The bottom line: By helping your clients set up employer-sponsored retirement plans, you can provide an important service to hundreds, if not thousands, of business owners and their employees.

Clearly, a void exists. Perhaps it's time to step up and fill it.

Once you understand your role clearly and fully, your decision to "take on the assignment" becomes easier to make. The following chapters will take you through many aspects of your role in the retirement plans business so ultimately you can decide what's right for you: to sell or not to sell retirement plans.

Your Assignment, Should You Choose to Accept It . . .

Employer-sponsored retirement plans are one of the few vehicles Americans have to actively and consistently save for their retirements. As a financial professional focused on the employer market, it makes sense to prospect at the smaller end of the market—companies with fewer than 1,000 employees—because larger corporations typically have well-established plans that rarely turn over.

Multiple service providers such as The Hartford offer a wide variety of products and vehicles for small- to mid-size companies. Because different plans offering various solutions exist, employers can feel overwhelmed. As a financial professional, you don't need to be an expert on retirement plans—as usual, your job is to expertly manage relationships with your clients. You'll work with your service provider to determine the best product choices and provide expertise on the details of the plan.

The bottom line: Your job is to manage the client relationship well.

2

RETIREMENT PLAN SALES— WHAT'S IN IT FOR YOU?

"There is very little difference in people, but that little difference makes a big difference. The little difference is attitude. The big difference is whether it is positive or negative."

–W. Clement Stone

As a financial professional, you recognize different ways to become successful and acknowledge many different definitions of success for your clients. If financial freedom defines *your* success, consider using employer-sponsored retirement plan sales as a primary marketing strategy—it's one of the best ways to achieve both short-term and long-term financial success.

Consider the possibilities for your practice. Although selling employer-sponsored retirement plans requires a different sales process than selling mutual funds, annuities, or securities to individual clients, this business opportunity represents a natural extension of your current skills, knowledge, and abilities.

As mentioned in Chapter 1, The Hartford's Retirement Plans Group teamed with *PLANSPONSOR* magazine in 2005 to survey financial broker/dealer firms and learn more about the opportunities and trends in retirement plan sales. Of the 46 firms that participated in this survey, 90 percent have seen a significant increase in retirement plan sales in recent years. Of the remaining

FIGURE 2.1 *Firms Taking Advantage of Retirement Plans Sales*

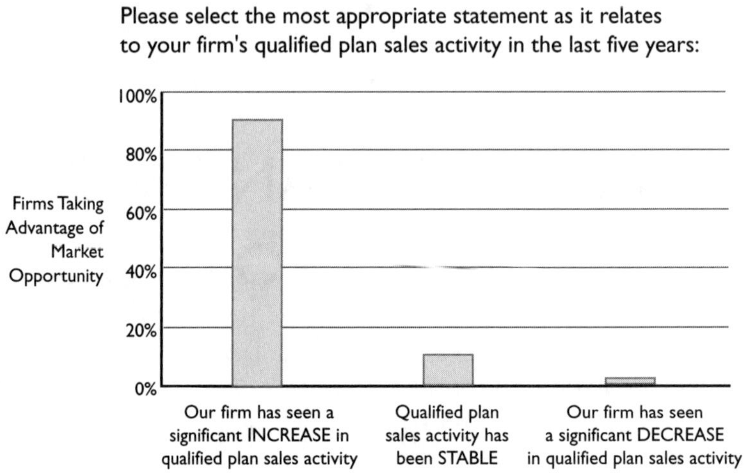

Please select the most appropriate statement as it relates
to your firm's qualified plan sales activity in the last five years:

| | Our firm has seen a significant INCREASE in qualified plan sales activity | Qualified plan sales activity has been STABLE | Our firm has seen a significant DECREASE in qualified plan sales activity |

Ninety percent of the financial broker/dealer firms that take advantage of the growing retirement plans market realized a significant increase in this sales activity in the past five years.

(Source: Survey conducted in 2005 by The Hartford's Retirement Plans Group and *PLANSPONSOR* magazine.)

10 percent, most sales activity has been stable; only an extremely small minority actually experienced a decrease in activity in the retirement plans market. These survey results underscore that the employer-sponsored retirement plans business is undeniably a market rich in opportunity and growth.

In case you haven't noticed, the days of having a guaranteed corporate pension plan or Social Security payout are fading fast. Today, individuals are expected either to plan for their retirement or deal with the consequences of having no money when they retire.

The overall statistics for retirement plans in the United States confirm this trend. According to the U.S. Social Security Administration, in 2004, people age 65 and older received only 39 percent of their income from Social Security and 19 percent from defined benefit pension plans. This means that 42 percent of their income was from personal savings or other personal resources. The legs of this three-legged stool—comprising corporate pension plans, Social

Security, and personal savings—will continue to become more unstable in years to come, particularly as baby boomers begin retiring.

Shifting retirement forces in America will continue to make the workplace a crucial area to address the retirement crisis. As the emphasis on retirement planning shifts away from corporate pensions and Social Security and toward employer-sponsored retirement plans, financial professionals are in a good position to help large numbers of people.

WHAT THIS CAN MEAN FOR YOUR PRACTICE

Now let's address your financial services practice specifically. Face facts: In your capacity, you have a limited ability to service a large number of people. Servicing 2,000 or 3,000 individual accounts isn't realistic. In fact, unless you're working with a large team, it's physically impossible. In reality, it's difficult to service more than 500 accounts while continuing to prospect for new ones. Yet offering employer-sponsored retirement plans as part of your service to clients can help bridge that gap.

Here are three solid reasons why building a retirement plans practice makes sense.

Reason 1: Ongoing repeat transactions with existing and new clients. With retirement plans business on the books for years, you would have an ever-growing, annuitized stream of income.

Employer-sponsored retirement plans can represent substantial asset growth potential over the long run. According to Cerulli Associates, the average ticket size for a small- to mid-size business's 401(k) plan is more than $5 million. Because retirement plans are built on periodic investments, their net income flow is steady and recurring, representing built-in revenue-generating opportunities for financial professionals.

Figure 2.2 illustrates the long-term compensation benefits of selling employer-sponsored retirement plans. If you sell just one $1 million plan every year for five years, your first year's commission of

FIGURE 2.2 *Long-Term Compensation Benefits*

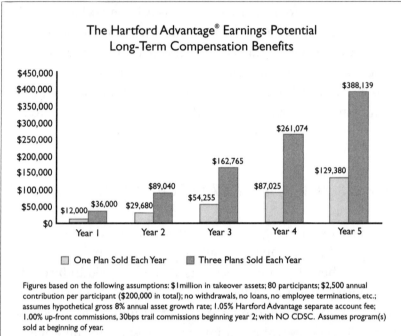

The Hartford Advantage® Earnings Potential
Long-Term Compensation Benefits

☐ One Plan Sold Each Year　　■ Three Plans Sold Each Year

Figures based on the following assumptions: $1 million in takeover assets; 80 participants; $2,500 annual contribution per participant ($200,000 in total); no withdrawals, no loans, no employee terminations, etc.; assumes hypothetical gross 8% annual asset growth rate; 1.05% Hartford Advantage separate account fee; 1.00% up-front commissions, 30bps trail commissions beginning year 2; with NO CDSC. Assumes program(s) sold at beginning of year.

This graph from The Hartford's Retirement Plans Group shows the long-term earnings potential for financial professionals selling retirement plans. If you sell just one $1 million plan every year for five years, your first year's commission of $12,000 grows to $129,380 in the fifth year. If you sell three plans a year, your commission in the fifth year is an astounding $388,139.

$12,000 can potentially grow to $129,380 in the fifth year. If you sell three plans a year, your commission in the fifth year could potentially grow to an astounding $388,139. This shows the value of doing business with retirement plans compared with completing one-time transactions. Plus, you have the potential to provide your services to a growing number of clients every year.

Notice that the chart in Figure 2.2 presents sales of only three retirement plans a year as the maximum example. Just think of your earnings potential if you sold more plans every year. As well, consider that many businesses have the potential to grow and take on additional employees; therefore, these companies' retirement plans may grow substantially. For example, a company with 200 employees may double to 400 employees in just a few years, potentially doubling the number of assets in the retirement plan—and your base commission. In addition, your opportunity to offer financial services to hundreds (if not thousands) of employees increases exponentially. There is a good chance that many of your plan participants hold significant assets beyond their employer-sponsored plan. Being associated with their employers' plans gives you a foot in the door to help these clients manage their financial goals and larger assets.

With a growing book of retirement plans business, you will get paid on ongoing contributions to the plans. This means you can spend less time marketing to mine new business and more time educating and servicing those in your client organizations (both business owners and plan participants). You'll help them grow their retirement assets while also possibly growing your own business. This opportunity has the potential to expand year after year.

Reason 2: Rollover business. Cement relationships with plan participants, and they'll look to you to roll over 401(k)s to individual IRAs, a potentially huge business opportunity.

As we noted above, studies have indicated that for every dollar held within an employer-sponsored retirement plan, the plan participants hold many more assets outside of their retirement plan account. Thus, providing retirement plans can be a great way to bring in assets much greater than a single plan itself. Imagine the potential increase for your business!

Becoming the financial professional of record on a retirement plan immediately puts you in a position of trust and credibility with employees who participate in the plan. This positions you to take advantage of one of the biggest opportunities in this business—rollover assets to individual IRAs as employees leave an organization or retire.

This opportunity can lead to a significant source of income, but it only happens if you're able to cement client relationships with trust. Here's an example of how this could happen. Two years ago, you sold an employer-sponsored retirement plan to ABC Company. Today, Joe Professional is leaving the company and needs to roll over his 401(k) to an individual IRA. You've done a good job cementing the relationship with ABC Company's employees like Joe, so it's only natural that he looks to you to roll over his 401(k) assets. Joe is 45 years old and has $300,000 in his 401(k). He's starting his own business, so he needs income and doesn't want to roll over all of his assets. After listening to what he wants to accomplish, you can provide Joe with financial guidance for solid distribution planning. As you know, every time you open a new product for Joe and other plan participants who come to you for financial services, you receive a commission check and a continuing annuitization.

If you don't cement the relationship with employees like Joe, however, other financial professionals have a good shot of getting those distribution dollars. According to requirement minimum dis-

---

What Baby Boomers Want from Their Financial Professionals

A June 2005 survey conducted by Mathew Greenwald & Associates, Inc. on behalf of The Hartford indicates that baby boomers are looking for a more holistic set of services from their financial professionals. According to the survey, titled *The Role of the Advisor in a Changing Retirement Marketplace*, the top three services boomers seek are:

1. help so they don't outlive their assets;
2. assistance with asset allocation; and
3. guidance in selecting the best investments.

But apparently baby boomers aren't getting what they want. When asked what services they were currently receiving from their financial provider, they ranked those needs in the opposite order.

The bottom line: Offering baby boomers the kind of service they need will keep them coming back for more services and products, earn you referrals, and potentially grow your business.

tribution rules, retirees must begin to withdraw a required minimum amount from IRAs, 401(k)s, and other plans at age 59½. The vast majority of these people will need financial professionals to help navigate their distribution phase because of ever-changing laws, regulations, and choices in plans and products.

Distribution planning promises to be the greatest opportunity created for financial planners. If you cement the relationships, you can help plan participants in the two most important phases in their lives: accumulation and distribution. In the next ten years, 78 million baby boomers have the potential to retire and enter the distribution phase. Cement relationships with the hundreds (or thousands) of plan participants during the accumulation phase, and they'll look to you for guidance in their distribution phase.

Figure 2.3 shows that in 2004, more than 70 percent of distributions from defined contribution plans were rolled over. Those who highly rate the performance of their investment representative tend to place 80 percent or more of their assets with that investment representative.

As Figure 2.3 indicates, capturing assets from employer-sponsored accounts plays directly into future opportunities to sell mutual funds, annuities, and IRAs. The percentage of assets in defined contribution (DC) plans that are rolled over into IRAs has been steadily increasing in recent years. As the financial professional of record for a company's defined contribution plan, you're in an ideal position to capture rollover assets for plan participants who either leave the company or decide to retire.

Notice one of this chart's main points: neither the rollovers nor the distributions from defined contribution plans (employer-sponsored retirement plans) are static—both amounts increase over time. As boomers begin to retire in record numbers, distributions coming out of retirement plans are increasing, and a significant percentage of those rollovers go to IRAs. These retirees have dutifully saved, and as a result, many may have $500,000 in their employer-sponsored retirement plans. Many of these retirees have never had a financial advisor, so when they retire, they look for help to roll over these monies into IRAs.

FIGURE 2.3 *Future Opportunity*

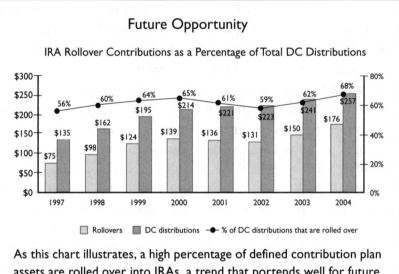

Future Opportunity

IRA Rollover Contributions as a Percentage of Total DC Distributions

	1997	1998	1999	2000	2001	2002	2003	2004
Rollovers	$75	$98	$124	$139	$136	$131	$150	$176
DC distributions	$135	$162	$195	$214	$221	$223	$241	$257
% of DC distributions that are rolled over	56%	60%	64%	65%	61%	59%	62%	68%

☐ Rollovers   ▨ DC distributions   ─●─ % of DC distributions that are rolled over

As this chart illustrates, a high percentage of defined contribution plan assets are rolled over into IRAs, a trend that portends well for future sales opportunities. Employer-sponsored retirement plans offer financial professionals excellent opportunities to reach retiring employees and help them navigate the distribution phase of their lives, as well as reaching employees who leave the company and want to roll over their assets into IRAs.

(Source: Mathew Greenwald & Associates, Inc., "Fertile Ground: Market Demand Drives Growth in Advisor-Sold Plans," 2005)

Remember, if you've been active and visible in the company's retirement planning process, you'll be the first person they look to for financial guidance—their number-one option.

Reason 3: Ancillary sales. Employer-sponsored retirement plans open doors for highly profitable ancillary business. Employer-based retirement plan sales can open up possibilities for additional profitable sales to other financial planning opportunities within the business environment. These might include health plans, deferred compensation plans, key person life insurance, buy-sell insurance, and estate planning opportunities for high-net-worth employees.

If you don't sell workplace retirement plans, these opportunities can be difficult to source, and once you find these clients, you would have to build strong relationships from the ground up. By offering employer-sponsored retirement plans and cementing relationships with plan participants, you can open doors to meeting these needs and selling these profitable products. In one real-life example, a financial professional sold a retirement plan to a small company with two owners. The plan was only $600,000. However, within the first year, the two owners gave this salesperson $10 million in ancillary sales.

We've presented three solid reasons to get started in the employer-based retirement plans business. You'll find many more as you explore the benefits of expanding your practice into this potentially lucrative market.

Todd's Story:
Two Real-Life Examples: Why Businesses Need Insurance

Ancillary business, particularly life insurance sales, offers huge opportunities to grow your business. When choosing your service provider, take time to have a serious discussion about ancillary sales. In fact, the number-one reason I entered the employer-sponsored retirement plans market was this: my top revenue-generating product was ancillary life insurance sales.

The following two examples illustrate how business insurance policies would have made a huge difference for two small companies.

Example 1: Key person insurance. This form of life insurance can be a cost-effective means of providing immediate liquidity to help a business recover from the death of a key employee, thus protecting the economic welfare of the company.

Years ago, I sold an employer-sponsored retirement plan to John and Bob. Two years earlier, John had gone to work for Bob. With complete confidence in John's abilities, Bob started spending more and more time in Florida. Bob never purchased key person insurance. This small manufacturing firm employed about 45 people. John was head of sales and plant manager. He applied everything he had learned from his mentor, Bob. Plus, he poured his youthful energy into the business and put creative ideas into place to expand the product offerings. The business thrived.

One evening on his way home from playing golf, John was hit head-on by a drunk driver and died. He left behind three children and a non-working spouse who was saddled with his debt. No one was left to run the company. Bob, the inactive business owner, was forced to come out of what had begun to feel like semi-retirement and take charge of the business. A lot had changed since Bob had been the "key" person running the company.

Bob felt like a fish out of water. And he was stressed. He strived to run the business while simultaneously trying to sell it. And he needed to arrive at a fair and equitable arrangement for himself and John's widow.

If Bob had purchased key person insurance to cover John's life, the policy would have lessened the impact created by John's loss and provided the funds necessary to offset the financial loss suffered by the company due to John's absence and the costs associated with recruiting John's replacement.

Example 2: Buy/sell insurance. Early in my career, I met with the partners of a firm that was recovering from a devastating situation. One of the partners (we'll call him Bill) had suffered a major stroke. After spending many months incapacitated in the hospital, he passed away. The surviving two partners had to buy out Bill's share of the business from his surviving spouse. This was a huge sum of money and the partners weren't prepared for this unexpected buyout. Ten years later, the company was still suffering from the adverse financial affects caused by Bill's passing. To make matters worse, Bill had been one of the company's top sales producers. Even if Bill had fully recovered after months in the hospital and returned to work, the company would have lost months of revenue.

If this company had purchased buy/sell disability and life insurance, it wouldn't have been burdened by this unfortunate event. Buy/sell insurance ensures a business's viability in case a partner, officer of the company, or top-producing salesperson becomes disabled or dies.

The bottom line: Employer-sponsored retirement plans open doors to profitable ancillary business, such as key person and/or death and disability insurance.

Thoroughness Is Key to Profitable Ancillary Business

For Kelly, a financial professional with a broker/dealer firm in St. Paul, Minnesota, a friend's 401(k) referral resulted in much more than a single transaction. The referral, a heating and cooling company with 80 employees, had an existing 401(k) plan with about $1.3 million in assets. The company's owner was impressed with the proposal Kelly prepared for a 401(k) plan from The Hartford, outlining the plan's multifund managers and low fees. But Kelly didn't stop there. This 401(k) plan got Kelly in the door, but her thoroughness and exceptional client service kept her on the inside.

As a standard bonus, Kelly offers participants a free will through a local attorney. She also offers every 401(k) participant and spouse a one-on-one financial profile. Additional discussions with the business owner had revealed a substantial need for life insurance. Kelly enlisted a colleague to help. Together, they wrote two policies—one for income replacement and debt reduction with a face value of $4.5 million and the other a second-to-die policy with a face value of $10 million.

The bottom line: Offer services your clients want to open the door; then spend time understanding their needs, filling them with a variety of services and products, and building lasting relationships.

3

NO MORE EXCUSES!

"A pat on the back is only 28 inches above a kick in the ass."
–John Crnokrak, The Hartford

You may be asking, "If employer-sponsored retirement plans provide such great opportunities, why don't all investment professionals market them?"

Let's look at several challenges financial professionals face when they sell retirement plans. Keep in mind that these perceived difficulties may scare off a majority of financial professionals, while offering excellent opportunities for those who choose to enter this market.

Challenge/Opportunity 1. Providing employer-sponsored retirement plans requires a longer sales cycle than selling individual retirement plans. To a certain degree, this challenge is true. It isn't likely you'd sit down with a prospect for a first-time meeting and close a sale right then. It is possible, however, to keep the cycle to 90 days or less. (Chapter 10 shows how to increase your closing ratio at your finals presentation, dramatically shortening your sales cycle.) With the increase of investor sophistication and the advancement of the Internet and other technology, the average sale time has decreased from more than 12 months to fewer than 3 months in recent years.

Challenge/Opportunity 2. Many financial professionals aren't comfortable selling and managing employer-sponsored retirement plan accounts. Perhaps you've never sold an employer-sponsored retirement plan before. If so, think of it as an extension of your current financial practice. It's possible that, due to the complexities of employer-sponsored retirement plans, you may be afraid of making costly mistakes, despite your experience in selling 401(k) and other individual retirement plans to clients. And learning a new sales process can be scary; as we noted earlier, employer-sponsored retirement sales require a different process than selling mutual funds, annuities, or securities to individual clients. We hope this book alleviates your concerns by providing step-by-step guidance to help you tackle our recommended Solutions Based Selling approach. Plus, you'll see how you can rely on your team of experts to provide plan specifics and help you win the business you want.

We encourage you to think of selling retirement plans as providing solutions rather than selling products. What types of solutions would you provide?

For employers, you help them provide future income for employees after retirement—generally a more cost-effective solution than offering pension plans. Plus, an employer-sponsored retirement plan is a positive benefit, helping the company increase retention and attract new employees.

For employees, you help them actively and consistently save for their retirement years. In most cases, employees save pretax dollars (or after-tax Roth dollars), saving on taxes now while saving for the future.

Needing to learn the details about these products shouldn't deter you. No one expects you to be a complete retirement plans expert. You can turn to a trusted and knowledgeable service provider to provide expertise in various aspects of plan design, administration, and service. You should view yourself as the client relationship expert on a full team of retirement plans experts. After all, you are the one person who knows the client's goals and objectives well enough to assemble the right team of people to serve your client's needs. (You will read more about assembling your team of experts in Chapter 7.)

Challenge/Opportunity 3. The closing ratio for selling employer-sponsored retirement plans is too low. Many financial professionals selling employer-sponsored retirement plans close approximately 30 to 40 percent of their business opportunities. This may sound low; however, the long-term profits and lucrative rollover and ancillary business (discussed in Chapter 2) prove that a batting average of 30 to 40 percent makes this business well worth your while. Plus, this business thrives on the team approach.

You Don't Have to Go It Alone

Due to the complexities of corporate retirement plan composition, ever-changing legislation, and the intricacies involving ERISA, the U.S. Department of Labor, and the Internal Revenue Service, your best interest lies in relying on the expertise of people who specialize in specific aspects of the retirement plans arena. They could be coworkers, home office professionals of your broker/dealer firm, or your service provider's local representatives. These people go through ongoing training on plan design, legislative issues, U.S. Department of Labor regulations, and U.S. Treasury policies and procedures. Their knowledge can help you identify solutions that lead to closing sales. Best of all, their services are usually free!

For example, The Hartford's Retirement Plans Group has more than 430 professionals located around the country—their number-one job is to work with financial professionals to provide sales, education, and enrollment support for retirement plans. This network of specialists will support your client relationship from initial sale and setup to ongoing service, administration, and education.

The bottom line: See yourself as the client relationship expert and rely on your team for specific areas of expertise.

As you'll learn in Chapter 7, your retirement plans specialist, third-party administrator, and other financial professionals in your broker/dealer firm add the experience and needed expertise to close business and raise your batting average.

Challenge/Opportunity 4. The corporate retirement plans marketplace is too competitive. In 2005, approximately 75,000 financial professionals sold some type of financial product from The Hartford. Of these same professionals, 2,500—only 3.3 percent—sold a company-sponsored retirement plan. This indicates a lot of room for growth in the retirement plans arena. In fact, we've arrived at an interesting time in the financial services history—a time when the *least* amount of competition overlaps with the *greatest* opportunity.

Challenge/Opportunity 5. Potential clients assume that retirement plans cost too much to implement. Small- to mid-size business owners are usually focused on making ends meet for

---

Which Profile Fits You?

At The Hartford, we've discovered that financial professionals enter the employer-sponsored retirement plan market at different stages in their careers and that just about any type of financial professional can be successful in this market. The keys are to work with a respected service provider, carefully select your team, build positive relationships with your clients, and focus on selling solutions, not products.

Which type of financial provider describes you?

Type 1: Experienced producer in other areas of business, but have sold only a few retirement plans. These professionals play it safe and conservative. They stick to what they know. They don't want to risk stepping outside the box and taking on something new—something that could reap much greater success but that could also net failure. Yet they want to generate a healthy growth in commission, perhaps discovering the key to an elusive earnings goal. They don't realize that the single best tool they have is *themselves*. When they realize that they are their number-one strength, they'll reach their peak potential.

Type 2: Inexperienced producer who has sold a few retirement plans. These financial professionals have enjoyed moderate success selling retirement plans. But they often get so excited about the ancillary sales these plans produce that they forget where the business comes from. They get focused on servicing individual participants (which, overall, is a good thing), but they fail to go after the next retirement plan. They don't realize that prospecting and selling employer-sponsored retirement plans needs to be part of their weekly business routine.

Type 3: Tried to sell retirement plans but failed and gave up. These financial professionals may have used sales techniques that are successful with their other products and services but didn't work for retirement plan sales. They met with failure and simply gave up too early. A healthy dose of patience and perseverance will help them succeed. These professionals need to muster the courage and commitment to stick with it. They'd be wise to live by this adage: "It's not practice that makes perfect. It's perfect practice that makes perfect." That means taking the time to analyze the right way to sell retirement plans, then going out and doing it the most effective way. This proves to be one of the differences between those who succeed and those who don't.

Type 4: Avoid selling retirement plans. Why avoid entering this potentially lucrative market? For many financial professionals, the underlying issue is comfort level. Other financial professionals may have told them that the monetary rewards are outpaced by the work required, the sales cycle is too long, or the market is too competitive. Or perhaps the issue is fear. They may feel confident selling other products and services but not retirement plans. Marc A. Silverman, CLU, ChFC, said, "The successful people discipline themselves to do what the unsuccessful people are unwilling to do."

The bottom line: Don't hesitate to take the next step in your career and enter the retirement plans market. Realize that *you* are your core product. Follow your natural ability to create strong relationships and get out of your comfort zone.

their businesses. As a result, they may consider a retirement plan to be too expensive to implement. In fact, a number of cost-effective ways exist for small business owners to implement plans that work for them. The potential benefits to the owners as well as their employees could far outweigh any start-up costs.

In the broad scope of employee compensation, retirement plans play a small part. In fact, according to U.S. Department of Labor statistics through 2003, on average, only 3.1 percent of overall employee compensation went into retirement savings. This is significantly less than the amount going to other benefits, most notably health insurance at 7.1 percent. As a retirement plans professional, you can help your clients see through their concerns to understand the benefits.

Challenge/Opportunity 6. Potential clients may fear that signing on to a retirement plan requires an ongoing commitment to that exact plan. Small business owners have heard all the negative stories about large corporations facing difficulty due to long-term pension commitments. They don't want to enter into an ongoing commitment they believe a retirement plan will entail. However, a well-constructed retirement plan scenario helps employers offer generous retirement plans for their employees without being saddled with an unwanted long-term commitment. You can overcome these objections by educating employers on how employer-sponsored retirement plans can play a positive role in their businesses.

Employer-sponsored retirement plans are another avenue for you to give value to your current business clients. If you already provide workplace retirement plans, how can you serve more businesses and grow your practice? Read on for ways you can accomplish these goals.

SOLUTIONS BASED SELLING: THE ROAD TO A SUCCESSFUL PRACTICE

4

WHAT IS SOLUTIONS BASED SELLING?

"What good is being the best if it brings out the worst in you?"
–Rodney Dangerfield

The Hartford's Retirement Plans Group follows a specific philosophy and approach to retirement plan sales that we believe can guide you, the financial professional, to a successful retirement plans practice. We call this approach Solutions Based Selling.

THE 80/20 RULE APPLIES TO SALES

You've heard of the 80/20 rule. It applies in many ways to sales. Our most experienced salespeople know that 80 percent of closing the sale is the ability to earn their prospects' trust and confidence. The other 20 percent comprises everything else: the product, price, competitor's pitch, and so on. If a prospect doesn't trust you or doesn't have confidence in your abilities, that prospect won't become your client.

How do you earn respect and trust so you can build prospects' confidence? Well, you could have a prolonged relationship with them, which takes months and even years. We suggest you build trust and confidence through Solutions Based Selling instead. This sales approach is based on having the courage to do what's right; having the commitment and integrity to care genuinely about your clients; and demonstrating these beliefs with honor, passion, and a dose of humility.

IT'S ALL ABOUT SOLVING PROBLEMS, NOT SELLING PRODUCT

At its core, Solutions Based Selling is about doing your homework and asking the right questions. The retirement plans market for small- to mid-size companies (fewer than 1,000 employees) is extremely diverse. Several service providers offer multiple plan designs featuring multiple products. Service providers typically offer approaches to help you identify the right solutions based on the needs of the employer. Although the retirement plans market is diverse and complex, as a financial professional, you don't need to have all the answers. You just need to ask the right questions and tap into the expertise of the service providers who'll help you locate opportunities and solve problems.

Don't Overlook 15 Percent of the Marketplace!

Who comprises a substantially large market segment for retirement plans? Employees of tax-exempt, not-for-profit 501(3)(c) organizations, including K–12 public schools and public universities. They also include social, religious, medical (hospitals, health care facilities, nursing homes), and a variety of charitable organizations.

Taken as a whole, these groups are often overlooked when it comes to planned retirement programs. Current plans available to these organizations tend to be overpriced. Plus, the organizations tend to be underserviced. As a result, employees are hungry for education and guidance on what's available and how it works. In many instances, the plan contracts don't allow the money to be moved; however, potential new regulations (see Chapter 2) would offer greater flexibility and the ability to transfer assets more readily. These conditions provide a real opportunity to financial professionals willing to provide the service these organizations need.

Until recently, the 403(b) was virtually the only choice for these not-for-profit organizations. While there are more choices available today, the 403(b) is still the most frequent choice of plans in this market segment. The 403(b) functions much like the 401(k): employees who participate in the plan designate a certain percentage of pretax dollars from their income to go into specific accounts (at the participants' direction). Upon retirement, they can draw from these funds for their retirement income.

So how does a financial professional break into the tax-exempt, not-for-profit market? As a whole, networking is the lifeblood of not-for-profit organizations. It's how they accomplish so much with their often limited budgets.

To be successful, financial professionals must network and actively form relationships. Do your homework and learn how to network within the nonprofit community.

Whom do you know who sits on a board of directors? Are you or your spouse active with any not-for-profit organizations? Do you financially support or have any other affiliation with religious or social welfare programs in your community? Do any of your clients serve on the boards of not-for-profit organizations?

To achieve success in this market, it's important to identify a plan provider dedicated to this market, because it requires unique services and support. Although many plan providers have dabbled in this arena and can provide contracts, products, programs, and services, few are truly committed to this market segment. For example, many providers only support a proprietary delivery mechanism. If you go to one of these companies for help, they can sell the case and take it away from you. You'll end up with just a finder's fee and miss out on the long-term, potentially lucrative ancillary business.

The bottom line: The nonprofit market is historically underserved. For financial professionals willing to learn about nonprofits and partner with the right plan provider, this market segment can be lucrative.

Another "Hidden" Opportunity: Municipalities Offer Potential to Grow Your Business

Often overlooked, the municipalities and instrumentalities market offers a surprisingly high number of salaried professionals hungry for financial guidance and assistance. This market includes government employees from the village, town, city, and state levels as well as employees who work in public safety (fire and police), public utilities (water, sewer, gas, and power), bridge and highway authorities, city and state hospitals, primary and secondary schools, and public colleges and universities.

The most common retirement products for this sector are 457 plans, which are similar to 401(k) plans for the private sector. However, it's important to note that 457 plans don't offer employer contributions, and enrollment must be voluntary.

As is often the case with government entities, the process for gaining new business differs from that in the private sector. Most large cities and state governments follow strict procurement laws. Decisions are often made by a deferred compensation committee comprising police and fire union representatives, representatives from other employee groups and unions, financial specialists, and often someone appointed by the mayor or governor. Committees generally make their selections through a request for proposal (RFP) process. Because of this procurement process, the sales cycle can be long—12 to 18 months. Committees generally choose only one provider.

If you discover that a bid process is underway in your community, you can ask to be invited to participate. If a bid process isn't underway, consider using a variety of techniques to encourage the municipality or instrumentality to open a bid process. For example, you may offer free financial planning and retirement preparation seminars to employees. (One idea is to offer seminars to on-duty firefighters in their firehouses; of course, you would be sure to get permission from management first.) During your investment seminars, you can discuss the 457 plan as one investment vehicle. You may even win over a "champion"—an employee who may influence the municipality or instrumentality to consider opening a bid and possibly selecting you as the financial professional on record for that organization's 457 plan.

The process for a small government entity including villages, towns, and small cities can be different than for a large one—and much simpler.

Often financial professionals are simply able to ask the town managers or treasurers to add their company's name to the list of 457 plan providers. It's then up to the financial professionals to differentiate their companies by providing top-notch, ongoing service.

Why pursue this market? For the same opportunities present in the private sector. Employees may hold significant additional income in other investments. This opens doors for significant potential ancillary sales. Plus, employees who leave may need to roll over assets into IRAs. Those nearing retirement may need direction for determining the distribution phase of their lives.

If you decide to pursue this market, do your homework. Take time to find the right plan provider with whom to partner. Beware: only six to ten providers are serious about this market. Therefore, make sure you address the following aspects for each of the companies you investigate:

- Financial stability
- Product flexibility
- Market commitment
- Sales track record
- Account retention rates
- Sales support and field structure
- Service history

The bottom line: Don't overlook working with governmental entities. This market segment can offer a wealth of opportunities.

GATHER INFORMATION AT THE START

We suggest you hire data-mining services such as Larkspur Data-Master Pro, Judy Diamond, and FreeERISA.com to help you get started. These services electronically sweep IRS Form 5500s—forms that are public record. Larkspur DataMaster Pro and Judy Diamond compile these forms in their databases. Using their search engines, you can learn key details for companies that currently have retirement plans. For example, if you live in San Diego, California, you can research companies' profit-sharing plans in San Diego or those in certain zip codes within and around that city.

The opportunities you can discover using these services are unlimited. Let's say you start with your existing book of business. Dr. Jones is a personal client of yours, so you look up his practice on Larkspur DataMaster Pro and see that he has an outdated money purchase retirement plan. You think he could benefit from one of the better retirement plan options available because of the EGTRRA law passed in 2001. This becomes the perfect opportunity to call him and ask him to meet with you and a retirement plan specialist from the provider of your choice.

You would start by asking to review his current retirement plan setup. Or, suppose Dr. Jones has a 401(k) plan but is having trouble putting away enough retirement dollars because he's failing the ADP (discrimination) test. (This situation happens with many employers.) In Dr. Jones's case, consider bringing in a specialist who can recommend ways to help meet this test. Your provider could present a variety of solutions such as automatic enrollment or a Safe Harbor plan (more about these later).

Maybe you've recommended a new retirement plan solution to clients who own small businesses, but they're hesitating to implement it due to perceived hassles and complexities. In these cases, you can also bring in an enrollment specialist to ease their concerns, boost their confidence in you and your team, and eventually win the business. (Having an enrollment specialist is a great asset to your team. When financial professionals bring in enrollment specialists for The Hartford plans, participation rates soar to more than 88 percent, creating solid foundations for successful plans.)

Remember: Don't limit your outreach to your existing book of business. Once you're comfortable with this research approach, you can use services such as Larkspur DataMaster Pro to find opportunities for employer-sponsored retirement plans throughout your region. Having this information at your fingertips makes it easier than you think to get started.

FIND THE HIDDEN GEMS

By proposing unique retirement plan solutions to small business clients in situations that make sense, you can distinguish yourself in this industry and build a successful practice. Just imagine the appreciation you'll gain from your small business clients when you help them implement a solution they never would have believed possible.

For example, small business owners who are older and more highly compensated than their employees may want to set up a retirement plan, yet they fear that they can't make an employer contribution in the company's lean years. This fear is unfounded. Current laws permit employers to set up profit-sharing retirement plans that allow discretionary employer contributions when appropriate. Therefore, in leaner years, the employer isn't obligated to fund the plan. Plus, by implementing alternatives such as age-weighted and new comparability plans, small business owners can potentially contribute more toward their own retirement funds without being discriminatory toward their employees. Here's how it can work.

Age-weighted plan. This plan is designed to benefit older, well-compensated employees because contributions are converted to equivalent benefits at retirement. Because older employees have shorter time horizons and generally receive higher salaries than younger employees, age-weighted plans allow employers to make larger contributions to older employees than plans that aren't weighted according to age.

New comparability plan. Similar to an age-weighted plan, the new comparability plan tends to favor well-compensated employees (in most cases, the business owner). Contributions are still converted to benefits at retirement, but in this case, employees are divided into groups based on the employer's funding objectives. Different employee groups can be funded in different ways, and these plans are designed to pass U.S. Treasury compliance testing rules.

Figure 4.1 shows an example of the value that creative plan design can offer an employer. Each scenario shows the same total contribution by the company owner. However, by using alternative plan designs, the company can maintain the owner's maximum contribution of $44,000 while reducing the cost of the plan from $68,000 (Scenario 1) to $50,000 (Scenario 4)—a savings of $18,000 for the business.

The first scenario in Figure 4.1 is a straight profit-sharing plan. In this plan, the business owner and each employee all receive an equal percentage of the profits, as dictated by law for this type of plan.

The plan in the second scenario uses an integrated formula. Because the owner makes more than $100,000 and isn't getting full Social Security withholding, this plan allows the company to put a greater percentage into the owner's profit-sharing retirement plan than allowed for other employees.

In the hypothetical situation in the third scenario, the business owner is older than rest of the company's employees. Therefore, this scenario allows the owner to receive a larger piece of total allocation, because the owner has a shorter time frame until retirement than the employees.

The fourth scenario uses a cross-testing plan, which takes into consideration the owner's age, compensation, and other variables. This combination of factors allows the business to contribute more money to the business owner. It isn't considered discriminatory because appropriate factors are involved.

FIGURE 4.1 *Hypothetical Profit-Sharing*

Hypothetical Profit-Sharing Design Scenarios

Participant	Age	Eligible Compensation	Scenario 1: Pro Rata		Scenario 2: Integrated		Scenario 3: Age-Weighted		Scenario 4: New Comparability	
			Allocation	%	Allocation	%	Allocation	%	Allocation	%
Owner	55	$220,000	$44,000	20.0	$44,000	20.0	$44,000	20.0	$44,000	20.0
Employee 1	20	$30,000	$6,000	20.0	$4,936	16.4	$900	3.0	$1,500	5.0
Employee 2	55	$30,000	$6,000	20.0	$4,936	16.4	$6,000	20.0	$1,500	5.0
Employee 3	40	$30,000	$6,000	20.0	$4,936	16.4	$1,765	5.8	$1,500	5.0
Employee 4	30	$30,000	$6,000	20.0	$4,936	16.4	$900	3.0	$1,500	5.0
Total Employer Contribution		$340,000	$68,000		$63,744		$53,565		$50,000	
% to Owner			64.7%		69.0%		82.1%		88.0%	

This hypothetical chart reveals the value that a creative plan can offer an employer. In the four scenarios, the business owner contributes the same amount of maximum contribution to the company's profit-sharing plan ($44,000). In Scenario 1, the company contributes 20 percent of the owner's salary as well as 20 percent of each employee's salary (according to this plan's rules) for a total employer contribution of $68,000. However, by using an alternative plan design—in this case, Scenario 4: New Comparability plan—the business maintains the owner's maximum contribution of $44,000 while reducing the cost for this profit-sharing plan from $68,000 to $50,000—a savings of $18,000.

How Reducing a Law Firm's Contribution Won a Retirement Plan and Opened the Door to $20 Million in Assets

Anthony Marshall, a SunTrust financial professional in Atlanta, Georgia, had spent several months trying to do business with the principals of an Atlanta-based law firm. Then he hit upon an idea to add value and win the firm's business: reduce the contributions the firm was making to its retirement plan.

Reduce contributions? Don't most high-net-worth individuals look for ways to make higher contributions to retirement plans? This particular law firm sponsored a profit-sharing plan with approximately $2 million in assets. Each employee received the same percentage of salary as a contribution to the plan. For example, each principal of the law firm received roughly $20,000 in contributions, equal to 10 percent of pay. This meant that all the other employees of the law firm also had to be given 10 percent of pay, resulting in a total contribution of $300,000.

Because the firm had three principal lawyers, the total contribution made to these principals was $60,000. In other words, the principals only received one-third of the total contribution.

Working with a Hartford retirement plans representative, Anthony was able to show the principals a new comparability plan design. New comparability plans are allowed under current regulations and can cause the majority of the total contribution to be made to older, higher-paid individuals—the profile of the principals. They determined that the principals' contribution of $20,000 each could be sustained under the new comparability design with a total firm contribution of $100,000—a savings to the firm of $200,000.

Not only was Anthony able to close the retirement plan, but because he demonstrated sophisticated planning skills, the principals of the law firm approached him about personal financial planning and wealth management as well. This opened the door to approximately $20 million in additional assets from the law firm's partners and their families.

The bottom line: The needs of some clients may not be immediately apparent, but taking time to uncover their needs can open the door to unforeseen business opportunities.

5

IT'S ALL ABOUT RELATIONSHIPS

"There has never been a better time to be a financial professional,
particularly one who focuses on retirement plans."

–Jim Davey, Senior Vice President and Managing Director,
The Hartford's Retirement Plans Group

Solutions Based Selling typically leads to forming complete, ongoing relationships between successful retirement plan salespeople and their clients. A shining example of someone who understands the power of relationships is Todd's grandfather. Todd's story shows how his grandfather mastered the "magic" of earning trust and respect.

"I remember as a young man growing up meeting many people who would instantly treat me like royalty as soon they found out who I was. Just five minutes earlier, the same person treated me as if I were just another guy. But five minutes later, someone had apparently sprinkled 'magic dust' over my head, knighted me, and proclaimed me to be of royal descent. Why? Because they found out I was a Thompson, but not just any Thompson, the son of my father, the nephew of my uncles, and above all, the grandson of my grandfather. The funny part is, my grandfather isn't royalty and isn't rich. And the only time I question whether he has 'magic dust' is in deer hunting camp when he always seems to bring home the biggest buck and win almost every card game.

"So why do people have that reaction? Because over the last 80-plus years of my grandfather's life (and so on with my father and uncles), he has earned the trust and respect of everyone who has ever met him. And believe me, it wasn't easy. My grandfather chose one of the most difficult career paths by becoming a service manager at a local car dealership. His job description read something like: *Service Manager—deal with people who are angry and blame you because their car is broken down and doesn't work properly. Enjoy the pleasure of informing them that you didn't hear the sound they were referring to, the car didn't demonstrate the problem they claim it has, and the repairs will take longer than expected and involve costs that require mortgaging their homes.*

"Somehow, my grandfather had a way of taking someone from extreme anger and frustration to a gleaming smile. His honesty, integrity, courage, and commitment to doing what's right has earned him a legendary status with anyone who has met him. People naturally assume that if I am a descendant of my grandfather, they can have trust and confidence in me as well.

"My father and my uncles are so different in every way that one would never guess they are in any way related—with this exception: they all bring a smile to anyone's face who is around them and they all have the trust and confidence of everyone who has met them. It's a dynasty that I'm proud to be a part of. While I may not be able to dance as well as my father (that may be a good thing, though) and I cannot make people laugh like he can, I do try to live up to our family's reputation.

"Whatever level of success I've had throughout my sales career boils down to earning the trust and respect of my clients. I haven't always been the most intelligent salesperson, I haven't always had the most superior product, and I haven't always had the least expensive product. Yet somehow, whether I was selling music equipment, automobiles, securities, or anything else, I have always excelled. There is no coincidence to this fact. You've heard of the 80/20 rule. This rule applies in many ways to sales. Many experts say that 80 percent of closing a sale is your ability to earn prospects' trust and confidence. The other 20 percent is composed of everything else.

If prospects don't trust you or don't have confidence in your abilities, they simply won't become your clients. I agree with this philosophy.

"Unfortunately, not everyone knows my grandfather, my father, or my uncles. Thus, I don't have instant credibility with everyone. More times than not, I have to earn their respect and trust and build confidence. How? Well, one method has been to build a prolonged relationship with prospects that gradually resulted in earning their trust and confidence. This could take months or even years. While my supervisors have always been some of the most fair and understanding employers I could have ever hoped for, I'm not sure any of them would've allowed me to have a 'cradle to grave' cycle (the time that spans from meeting a prospect to closing the sale) that takes months or years. Thus, I'm challenged—like any other salesperson—to find a way to establish trust and confidence in hours, or even minutes.

"How do you do that, you ask? By using Solutions Based Selling. This approach is based upon the simple fundamentals of having the courage to do what's right, having the commitment and integrity to truly care about the customer, and demonstrating these beliefs with a dominant honor and passion—just like my grandfather has done for his entire life."

The keys to your sales success are earning clients' trust, gaining their confidence, and helping them solve problems. And you can do this by using Solutions Based Selling. The "selling" part of this phrase is really a misnomer, because this approach is first and foremost about establishing and maintaining relationships with clients. In this relationship, you're regarded as a trusted professional—someone who solves problems rather than sells widgets.

The idea of becoming a trusted professional cannot be stressed enough. Your clients will look to you for answers and guidance concerning their fiduciary responsibilities and to create an investment policy statement. (See the model investment policy statement in Appendix 2.) Your ability to provide answers will enhance your relationship with those clients.

While this process is about establishing personal connections, developing relationships means taking a systematic approach to learning the challenges your clients face and taking steps to solve their challenges.

HOW TO CREATE A FOUNDATION OF TRUST

Developing solid relationships, winning confidence, and establishing trust: a tall order. How do you do it in a reasonable amount of time during your sales process? Again, use Solutions Based Selling.

Here are four steps to taking a Solutions Based Selling approach from the beginning.

Step 1: Prepare for your finals presentation. This sounds obvious, but not everyone does it. Invest time to research your prospects and their organizations. Get to know everything about their history, their culture, and their products and services. Many companies have Web sites, and you can locate countless printed publications online through search engines or in hard copy at the public library. A company's annual report is an excellent source of information on the company, its key officers, core strategies, and affiliated businesses. If the company isn't publicly listed and doesn't have an annual report, find someone in the company who can be a good source of insight for you. (See Chapter 9, which presents essential guidance on the importance of preparation.) The key is this: by studying this information, you can show employers that you understand their challenges.

Step 2: Before your presentation, make sure you understand what your clients want to accomplish at the meeting. They may already have selected you, and you could risk overselling your way out of a sale. They may have a different agenda than what you thought or expected. Ask questions to identify what's important to the clients and make sure you fully understand why. This approach also shows that you are focused on solving their particular challenges, not just going through a canned presentation.

Step 3: Be flexible. Typical finals presentations might be directed to an audience of three people: the CEO, the human resources director, and the person in charge of payroll. All three likely have different agendas, personalities, and needs. That's why it is important to be flexible. Have your formal presentation ready, but also go in with a blank flipchart. At the start of the meeting, ask each person to list key wants, needs, and concerns relating to the ideal employer-sponsored retirement plan. Write these down and refer back to them during the presentation to make sure you address each one specifically. Now you're more than a salesperson; you're a problem solver. (Chapter 10 addresses this approach in more detail.)

Step 4: Ask for the order. If you have gone through the steps already noted, then asking for the business should be a given—a slam dunk. What do we mean by this? After you assessed your potential client's challenges and explained how you can address all those challenges, you need to ask for the sale. One approach is to ask your audience: "I've answered all your questions and addressed all your challenges. Is there any reason you won't sign us as your retirement plans provider?"

Regardless of what answer you hear, you'll have a better idea of where you stand than you did at the beginning of the meeting. You need to leave the room with a good idea of whether you won the business, lost the business, or are still in the hunt. And if you receive follow-up questions from the employer after the meeting, be sure to respond as soon as possible. If, after the meeting, you hear that a competitor edged you out, ask for the chance to address what they may think you missed. Better yet, if possible ask the clients to let you know *before* the final decision if they have questions you didn't address. You may actually have a great answer for them, but for some reason the topic didn't come up in your presentation. You'll learn more about this critical sales step in Chapter 10.

Once you've won the sale, you can continue to earn the client's trust and confidence—and differentiate yourself from other financial professionals—by educating your clients whenever new options become available or changes in retirement plan laws occur. An example is the Roth 401(k), which became available January 1, 2006. This 401(k) feature allows employees to contribute post-tax dollars to their 401(k) plans, creating a tax-free source of income at retirement. The Roth 401(k) may or may not be right for certain employers and their employees. The choice should be based on a number of factors related to compensation, retirement time horizon, and tax status. Because this option may be attractive to employees who are nearing retirement, you could present this feature to employers who have an older workforce and educate them on the pros and cons of this feature. In addition, the Roth 401(k) may be attractive to highly paid individuals because, unlike the

What Employers Want from Their Financial Professionals

Take note of this feedback from employers who have 401(k) programs using a financial professional (from *PLANSPONSOR*/The Hartford Financial Advisor Survey, September–October, 2003):

- *Be an advocate.* Employers want to hear your ideas and see a plan for acting on them.
- *Be visible.* Take time to meet members of the entire management team, not just the owner.
- *Earn their trust.* Show participants you have their best interests in mind.
- *Tailor your messages.* Vary your messages to be more topical or age based. Don't just focus on the basics.
- *Focus on the big picture.* Encourage participants to look at their investments holistically, not just at their 401(k) account.
- *Be available to everyone.* Regardless of account size, everyone has a vested interest in attaining a comfortable retirement.
- *Stay there.* Help retirees ease into a transition period. Be available when they need you most.

The bottom line: Providing employer-sponsored retirement plans isn't a "done-and-run" business. Plan to deliver ongoing support. Plan, too, for long-term profits.

Roth IRA, there are no income limitations. Plus, it may be attractive for young employees who believe they will be in a higher tax bracket when they retire.

As a financial professional, you can differentiate yourself as a resource to your clients by providing education on this option and suggesting whether (or when) this option might make sense for their plan.

BUILDING LOYALTY BY HELPING EMPLOYERS ADDRESS FIDUCIARY CONCERNS

Fiduciary concerns can be a primary stress point for employers when it comes to retirement plans. As a financial professional, you can position yourself as a real consultant to employers by helping them work through the fiduciary guidelines. Meanwhile, you can build relationships by educating them on their fiduciary responsibilities and providing support to ensure they're in compliance.

It isn't necessary for you to know the myriad legal details relating to ERISA. When you select a service provider (such as The Hartford), that provider will help make you look like the expert. It's in the service provider's best interest to educate you and ensure you look smart in front of your clients. And, of course, if you need to reference legal details, you can simply call your service provider to understand this information better. (Chapter 7 gives you guidelines on how to build your team, starting by selecting a service provider that will stand with you and help you to win, educate, and retain clients.)

But you do need a general understanding of ERISA. Its primary purpose is to impose specific duties on plan fiduciaries. According to the Act, a plan fiduciary must act in the best interests of plan participants and beneficiaries to ensure that the plan provides the benefits due the participants and defrays reasonable plan expenses.

A fiduciary must:

- Act with care, prudence, and diligence
- Diversify the investment options of the plan to minimize the risk of large losses

- Act in accordance with the documents and instruments governing the plan

Fiduciary responsibility carries a great deal of potential liability for employers if they improperly manage their retirement plans. Unfortunately, most employers don't have the proper knowledge to meet these responsibilities, and they don't fully understand the magnitude of the potential liability. According to ERISA, "A person who breaches any of the responsibilities, obligations, or duties imposed upon fiduciaries by this title shall be personally liable to make good to such plan any losses to the plan resulting from each such breach . . ."

Employers are also often confused about who the plan fiduciaries are. ERISA spells this out as well. Generally speaking, plan fiduciaries:

- Exercise discretionary authority and/or control over the administration of the plan
- Have discretionary authority or discretionary responsibility in the administration of the plan
- Exercise authority and/or control over the management or disposition of plan assets
- Give investment guidance to the plan participants for a fee or other compensation, whether direct or indirect.

Appendix 2 contains a list of questions that you can review with employers to ensure that they are in compliance with ERISA. Appendix 3 includes a checklist of items your clients should include in a due diligence file to avoid ERISA violations and create a positive framework for the plan.

Many Employers Are Unaware of Their Fiduciary Responsibilities

The following chart shows evidence that employers feel unsure about what's expected of them in the role of fiduciary.

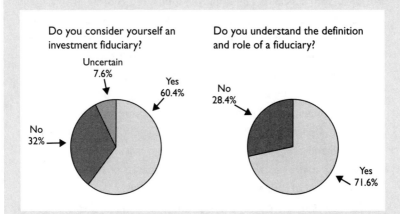

When it comes to fulfilling fiduciary obligations, a PLANSPONSOR/ Hartford Research Study (November 2003) provided insight into two key questions: whether employers consider themselves fiduciaries and whether they understand the definition and role of a fiduciary. While many respondents stated they understood what the responsibilities entailed, a surprisingly high number were either "unsure" or "unaware" of their fiduciary obligations.

The bottom line: Clearly, confusion exists surrounding the fiduciary (financial) responsibilities of plan sponsors. Knowing this offers an opportunity for financial professionals to provide service, educate employers, and possibly garner new business.

Building Trust and Business by Educating Fiduciaries

Tom Noble, owner of Noble Retirement Group, serves the Houston area from his Sugar Land, Texas office. As an independent financial professional, Tom specializes in employer-sponsored retirement plans and has become an expert in fiduciary responsibilities. He offers a unique—and successful—approach to educate business owners about their fiduciary responsibilities. This approach opens doors to new business opportunities for his firm. His words of explanation follow.

"I've witnessed a shift in the role of the financial professional when it comes to selling and supporting employer-sponsored retirement plans. In the past, more emphasis was placed on building investment menus and educating participants. While this is still important, I've found that the emphasis has shifted to those in charge of the business and those in charge of retirement plans: the fiduciaries.

"Business owners and managers must understand their roles and responsibilities—what they should have been doing as fiduciaries and what they need to do going forward to protect themselves. To help educate them, we sponsor monthly lunch seminars at one of Houston's nicest restaurants. We educate business owners on their roles and responsibilities and ensure they're aware of their exposure.

"How did I get educated? By completing Don Trone's program offered through the Wharton School of Business. Trone, a noted expert in the field, is president of the Foundation for Fiduciary Studies and is the founder and director of the Center for Fiduciary Studies. Financial professionals who complete the course receive a designation of Accredited Investment Fiduciary.

"As an Accredited Investment Fiduciary, I invite fiduciaries to a one-hour luncheon seminar to explain just what their role is and the scope of their exposure. While Don Trone is working with Congress to draft a standard of care for fiduciaries, currently no governing body tells fiduciaries what they're supposed to do. And make no mistake—fiduciaries do have responsibilities and exposures.

"Here's an example to illustrate the seriousness of the fiduciary role. A disgruntled employee who's lost a large sum of money in a company's retirement plan can sue the fiduciary *personally* on the grounds that the fiduciary didn't properly educate the employee. This is a sobering thought for anyone at the company who is responsible for the retirement plan.

"How can fiduciaries protect themselves? They can:

- Document practices in the investor policy statement
- Have a system in place to monitor the funds on a quarterly basis so a poor fund doesn't remain in the menu without being detected and replaced
- Offer plan participants education and guidance from a licensed professional
- Benchmark the plan at today's pricing

"At the lunch seminar, we extend a free offer to benchmark the employers' plans and rate the plans' funds based on performance. We begin the process by reviewing a company's plan performance over time. To determine this, we use a scoring methodology software that allows us to rank each fund against its entire peer group. The goal, of course, is to ensure that the business's retirement plan offers best-in-class funds. Also, we research whether the plan is priced competitively. And we look at the fund distribution: Does the distribution appropriately cover the style boxes—large cap, mid cap, small cap, value, domestic growth funds, international funds, bonds, value funds, money markets, and so forth? Through our free benchmarking service, we find that most companies are unaware that they have underperforming funds, an expensive plan, or poor style box coverage.

"The importance of benchmarking the plan can't be stressed enough. Here's an example. An employer was paying $18,000 a year in hard-dollar costs to sponsor the company's retirement plan. The business owner took advantage of our offer to benchmark the company's plan. The result? A more flexible plan with no hard-dollar costs and better-performing funds.

"Clearly, benchmarking is an important component of our prospecting activity. Prospecting begins when we invite employers to our luncheon seminar. We provide valuable information to them and begin to earn their trust by explaining their responsibilities and letting them know what they should be looking for in their plan. Our goal isn't to do a conversion; our goal is to fix the plan they're in. As a result, they hire us to be their financial professionals going forward. In addition to gaining new clients, we're educating our public. We know how to protect them, and if they hire us to manage their retirement plans, it's a win-win situation.

"Currently one of my large clients is going through a Department of Labor audit. We know that those involved are prepared because we helped them compile their Investment Policy Statement, all the documentation regarding how they made investment decisions, and minutes from all committee meetings. Most fiduciaries aren't aware of this, but they're required to have this information and keep the documentation up to date. Our office stores the documentation electronically so we can provide it to our clients in the event of an audit. This is another example of value-added service we provide to our clients."

The bottom line: Fiduciaries are required to understand their roles and responsibilities. As a financial professional, you are in a unique position to educate fiduciaries and possibly gain new clients in the process.

THE LIFE CYCLE OF RETIREMENT PLAN SALES: DO'S, DON'TS, AND LESSONS LEARNED

6

PROFILING YOUR
TARGET MARKET

"It's not the will to win that matters—everyone has that.
It's the will to prepare to win that matters."

–Paul "Bear" Bryant, one of the greatest college football coaches of all time

The first step to develop your retirement plans practice is to assess and develop your target market. Where is the most opportunity? What is your specific area of expertise? What is your market of greatest opportunity?

As you may have realized in the Introduction, Todd is an avid fisherman. The following story illustrates why selecting your target market is critical.

"Growing up, my grandmother spent a great deal of time with me. She taught me how to fish, she taught me how to cook, and she taught me the value of taking care of my family and other people as well. She instilled these and other values in me as I grew from a boy to a man (although my wife would argue that there is still way too much boy left inside of me). One of my memories of my grandmother involves a trip to Dunbar, Wisconsin. It was my first trip to the cabin my grandparents had built with their own hands. My grandmother took me fishing in a nearby community pond.

"The first fish I caught was a glimmering beauty—extraordinary in size, girth, and colors. Unfortunately, it was a rainbow trout and I didn't have a trout license. It didn't matter that it was truly a trophy catch. It was the wrong fish!

"My grandmother insisted I return the trout to the water. As a young boy, throwing the biggest and most beautiful fish I had ever caught back into the water seemed impossible, inappropriate, even *wrong*. But she was right. So we returned the fish back to the waters it came from and continued fishing.

"Sometimes what appears to be the obvious trophy—or greatest opportunity—is nothing more than a distraction if you don't catch the right fish."

As a financial professional, you must strategically pack your "tackle box" with the best "lures" to catch the right "fish" so you don't waste time working with clients who aren't the right fit for your business. So first, determine exactly what you're fishing for: Who is your target market? Second, identify where you'll be fishing: Where is your target market located (for example, your local region, statewide, or nationwide)? Third, you need to know what they're biting: What problems can your solutions help solve?

Take time to prepare a strategic and tactical approach to your marketing efforts. Determine your target market and then stick to it. Other perceived "trophy catches" can prove to be time-consuming distractions.

DEFINE YOUR TARGET MARKET

The first action to take is to identify what you're fishing for: Who is your target market? Perhaps your target market is within a geographic area, such as a variety of small- to mid-size businesses within your local region. Or perhaps your target market doesn't have geographic limitations because you plan to focus on a specific sector such as the health care industry, grocery stores, or school districts. Perhaps you prefer to target a sector in which you have career experience. They key is to determine where you want to focus your energy and the type of companies with which you're comfortable working. Are you a muskellunge fisherman with the patience to target this large freshwater trophy fish? Or do you want fast success by aiming to catch a panfish? In other words, do you have the patience to pursue larger, difficult-to-win clients that can lead to large profits? Or do you prefer to work in a specific target market that may yield more frequent wins, albeit smaller catches.

You may have already established an area of specialty in your current financial practice. For example, you may handle the personal portfolios for a number of doctors, lawyers, or contractors. This could be a natural starting point for your employer-sponsored retirement plans practice.

Whatever your sales strategy, you'd be wise first to establish your priorities. Target the areas in which you have an interest and will find enjoyment. To properly strategize this step, create a written document that identifies your target market. Doing this could be as easy as saying, "I'm fishing for panfish."

WHERE IS YOUR TARGET MARKET LOCATED?

Once you select your target market, identify where you'll be fishing to make sure you've selected a proper species (target market). It won't do you much good to fish for walleyes where walleyes are rare. In other words, perhaps you want to target lumberyards because your father worked in a lumberyard, you had summer jobs at lumberyards, or you like the smell of America's most renewable resource. This may or may not be a wise choice, depending on whether you'll be working in an area with a sufficient supply of lumberyards. If you're looking to market in downtown Chicago, for instance, you may struggle to find a sufficient number of lumberyards to catch enough "fish" for dinner, and you'd be better served redefining your target market. As another example, if you love computers and want to target technology companies, you'll struggle to find these in rural areas.

Also, are you more likely to catch your target market in certain climates? Are you focusing on a target market that may be struggling in today's economic climate and thus is looking for solutions to find needed relief? Will your target market be ready and willing to hear about your solutions? Will you be passing on cost savings? Improving morale among participants? Or would you find that you're fishing in the wrong weather conditions?

Perhaps you want to provide solutions to companies experiencing tremendous growth and earnings. You could provide solutions to meet these companies' specific needs. In any event, you need to know what's going on with the species of fish you're after. You need to know whether they're in a prosperous cycle, retracting cycle, or experiencing a plateau before or after a rise. Make sure your target market is inclined to make changes in today's economic climate.

Are you fishing on sunny days with crystal-clear water or cloudy days with murky water (that is, is the market heading up or down)? Do you think the market's perceived strength, its movements, or its momentum may have an impact on whether your prospects are willing to make a change? Make sure you find out how your prospects feel about today's market climate.

Are you targeting employers that may be motivated to change their program due to articles appearing in newspapers, magazines, or on television? These media campaigns—positive and negative, realistic and "witch hunts"—have an effect on decision makers. Make sure you understand how the media influences your prospects' decisions.

Finally, ask yourself: Why should my prospective client do business with me instead of my competitors? To differentiate yourself from your competition, you can develop a mission statement detailing the services you provide. Sign your mission statement and give a copy to prospective clients.

WHAT ARE YOUR PROSPECTIVE CLIENTS' PROBLEMS?

Whether you're appealing to businesspeople you already know or to those in a profession unfamiliar to you, do your homework.

We suggest you look around and identify relatives and good friends in the professions you're targeting. Then, over a cup of coffee, ask them to share their business concerns so you can get in tune with how they think.

For example, say your mother is an attorney. Sit down with her and ask probing questions to get insight into how most attorneys regard financial issues. Similarly, if your uncle is a contractor and you want to target businesses in the construction industry, ask how he makes his financial buying decisions. These casual interviews will help you identify workable approaches to take with your target market.

In the course of the conversation, your mother and uncle could give you valuable references or introductions. As you can see, even casual conversations with friends and relatives can help you learn about your target market. Take the next step and set up practice

---

Contact Those in Your Book of Business for a Regular Checkup

Take a cue from something dentists do extremely well; they schedule their patients for regular checkups. The dental industry has set a standard for doing this, and so can financial professionals.

As you begin to define your target market for employer-sponsored retirement plans, consider starting with your current business owner clientele. After all, they've already placed their trust in you. Plus, you probably regard your current book of business as your comfort zone. So set up regular financial checkups with these clients; this is an excellent place to start when introducing employer-sponsored retirement plans.

Ask these clients, "What do you like most about your current plan? What do you like least about your plan? If I can show you a way to improve or eliminate the negative aspects of your current plan, would you be interested in pursuing this conversation?"

The bottom line: Setting up financial checkups with current clients is a good place to start prospecting for workplace retirement plans and expanding your services.

presentations with those references. You will have an excellent opportunity to hone your skills, and you might win the business.

Next, conduct research to learn more about your target market. Read articles on the Internet, subscribe to trade publications, and attend industry trade shows. Your goal is to understand the targeted organizations' overarching business concerns, not just specific concerns relating to employer-sponsored retirement plans.

Invest the necessary time to create a complete profile of your target market. Your well-researched profile is the dock from which you'll launch your retirement plans practice.

7

BUILDING YOUR TEAM

*"You can get everything in life you want
if you will just help enough other people get what they want."*
–Zig Ziglar

Today, you rely on your expertise and sales ability to provide financial services to your clients. You provide a variety of products and services to help them meet their financial goals. At times, you may team with other financial providers in your broker/dealer firm to shore up areas in which you have less expertise.

To sell employer-sponsored retirement plans, you'll want to take this team concept a step further. Without question, this business requires a team that will likely include:

- *Service providers.* Your associate in the retirement plans business, service providers are the insurance companies (such as The Hartford) that provide a variety of employer-sponsored retirement plan designs, assist in the sales process, and offer ongoing client service. In reality, when you choose a service provider, your decision will depend more on the quality of the retirement plans specialist (often referred to as a regional sales manager) than on the company's product mix.

- *Third-party administrator.* Your associates on the administrative and record-keeping front, these accountants specialize in compliance testing to help ensure companies meet their fiduciary requirements for retirement plans. Some service providers (such as The Hartford) offer this service in-house, some providers have created business relationships with companies that provide third-party administrative services, and some providers offer a combination of these two strategies. Once you select the service provider, the retirement plans specialist can offer guidance to select the third-party administrators who will complement your team.
- *Other financial professionals.* You sometimes may wish to partner with other professionals in your broker/dealer branch offices or corporate headquarters for certain client presentations. For example, someone on your team may be an expert closer. Someone else on your team may offer a wealth of knowledge about providing ongoing education to employers to support their fiduciary responsibilities.

Your goal is to surround yourself with the resources you need to be competitive. Most of all, you want to find the right provider and retirement plans specialist to help you strategize, sell, advise on evolving laws and trends, and provide ongoing client support. This chapter helps you determine how to partner with the right service provider and build your service team.

SELECT A SERVICE PROVIDER THAT SUITS YOUR NEEDS

How do you determine which service provider is best for you? Of course, the company's product offerings and quality of service are critical. More important, however, is the retirement plans specialist, who is in a position to:

- Help you win business
- Help you retain business

- Help you gain ancillary business through good service (retirement plans can open doors to life insurance sales, rollover IRAs, and other profitable opportunities)

Questions to ask of the service provider:

- How will this provider help you devise a marketing strategy?
- What is the provider willing to do to help market employer-sponsored retirement plans?
- What role will this provider have in your sales process?
- What role will the provider play in helping you maintain plans and retain clients after the sale?
- What is the provider's retention rate?
- What will the provider do to assist you in marketing and building ancillary business?
- What are the strengths and weaknesses of particular providers with respect to their reputation and appeal to participants?
- From an employer's point of view, what are the strengths and weaknesses of each provider?
- What type of employer would favor the plan designs this provider offers?
- What areas may raise concern or prevent you from closing prospects with this provider's services and products?
- What value does the employer get for the cost? Remember, there is much more to a plan than cost and the characteristics and numbers of funds available.
- What do you and the employer get in the form of education, enrollment support, Web site resources, customer service, toll-free telephone assistance, and assistance in the fiduciary and due diligence processes?

When interviewing a prospective provider, make sure you discover whether the company's business is growing, how much revenue it brings in, its retention rates, and how many plans the company loses each year.

Take a look at the direction of each provider's business model: Is it up or down? Find out how long each provider has consistently provided employer-sponsored retirement plans. Does it have a history of entering and exiting the retirement plans marketplace? And beware: some providers' products are designed to help you put new business on the books but aren't designed to help you retain business. Keep in mind that long-term retention and ancillary business opportunities are hallmarks of the employer-sponsored retirement business. Again, you should partner with a service provider that helps you win and retain business while offering products that increase opportunities for profitable ancillary sales.

Does the Provider Offer Continuing Education? Listen to Client Concerns?

When selecting a service provider, take time to learn how the service provider communicates with its financial professionals. For example, The Hartford sponsors a Successful Selling Seminar Series, regular conference calls designed to educate financial professionals about new laws, regulations, trends, and more. The company trains individual broker/dealer firms on how to sell employer-sponsored retirement plans using the Solutions Based Selling approach. Plus, it offers continuing education courses for financial professionals and even conducts seminars on behalf of financial professionals for their clients regarding specific changes in laws or regulations.

Also, partner with a service provider that listens to its customers. As an example, one of The Hartford's ways to listen to its customers is to hold focus groups with financial professionals from top financial broker/dealer firms. The Hartford presents planned product changes and enhancements, basically saying, "Here's what we're thinking of producing. Now what do *you* think?" The Hartford's employees leave the room and ask the clients to discuss what The Hartford is doing right or wrong and what's lacking. The Hartford people return to the room and listen to their clients' feedback. Quite often, this feedback results in specific changes to product offerings.

The bottom line: Partner with a service provider that helps you get up and running smoothly and provides education to the employees, too.

Also, ensure that the provider will support you with retirement plans specialists—professionals who are trained in the procedures and regulations to put together plans correctly. Perhaps you aren't used to relying on this resource for most of the products you offer. For example, you don't usually call wholesalers or company representatives to help you sell stocks, bonds, annuities, or mutual funds. For employer-sponsored retirement plans sales, however, you're better off relying on specialists than learning the entire process on your own. You'll achieve much more than if you risk limiting the value you can bring to your clients.

Finally, when selecting a service provider for your team, think about matching your expert support to your target market. A well-chosen expert can provide instant credibility in a sales setting. For example, if you're prospecting law firms, does the service provider have a lawyer available to attend your finals presentations? By the

---

Service Providers' Retention Rates: Check These Numbers Carefully

How can you measure ahead of time the quality of service you're likely to get from a service provider? By finding out the company's retention rate—the percentage of clients who renew their agreements or products. Obviously, the higher the number, the better.

But it's not that simple. You need to clarify which components have been calculated into the published retention rate. Specifically, find out if the rate reflects deferred sales charges (an amount charged when a client cancels the company's product). Only consider service providers that demonstrate high retention without folding deferred sales charges into their numbers.

To gain a client's business and overcome the objection of paying down these deferred charges, some companies (including The Hartford) will take over the former company's deferred sales charge and roll it into the new contract. It's important to know if your service provider will provide this option before you sign on with that provider.

The bottom line: Be sure to check and fully understand service providers' retention rates. After all, this impacts *your* long-term business.

same token, a CPA can add credibility if you're targeting accounting firms.

Although having these professionals available may be useful, keep in mind that the most important factor to consider when selecting a service provider is the retirement plans specialist. Which provider's retirement plans specialist will support your business? Do you trust this person to get you to the next level in your career as a retirement plans professional?

BE YOUR OWN TEAM LEADER

More so than any other financial product, the sales process and ongoing service for a retirement plan involves much more than just you. This business is about assisted sales. Yet if something goes wrong in the service of your plan, it will reflect on you and only you. Therefore, it's important that you act as a team leader. Early in the sales process, clearly identify your role and the roles of your team of experts. When you present your solution to an employer, introduce each of your team members and clearly, concisely explain their roles on your service team. This approach helps to set clear expectations with your prospects before they become customers and helps make your client relationships run smoothly from the start.

Service Is King: You Own the Client Relationship

The average employer-sponsored retirement plan changes its provider every three to five years. The most common reason for making this change isn't how well the investments perform; it's poor service. When you select a service provider and third-party administrator, take time to understand and discuss the level of service they'll provide for your clients. You want to ensure that the provider and third-party administrator will continually offer good service, putting you in the best position to retain the plans you sell.

What defines poor service? This catch-all term could mean that company representatives haven't heard from the financial professional for a long time—too long. Perhaps the third-party administrator doesn't meet deadlines, and the financial professional refuses to iron out the issues. Perhaps the service provider doesn't mail statements on time; again, the financial professional is absent from the picture and isn't working with the provider to help resolve the issue. Perhaps employees aren't sufficiently educated to make informed decisions. This lack of education affects the company's fiduciary responsibility; the employer feels left out in the cold and vulnerable to lawsuits.

At the center of each scenario is the financial professional, who must have a pulse on the company's retirement plan and consistently provide a high level of service. After the sale, the financial professional and the team, which often includes enrollment specialists, help with the initial enrollment meeting, hold periodic reviews with the employer's day-to-day administrator to meet targeted participation rates, attend annual meetings with participating employees, help educate employees about allocation options, and assist the employer in meeting its fiduciary responsibilities.

The bottom line: Providing service offers both a challenge and an opportunity for you. Your challenge: Deliver a high level of service to retain your clients and win ancillary business. Your opportunity: When other financial providers don't service their clients well, employers looking for a change will welcome your solutions and high-level service.

8

PROSPECTING FOR CLIENTS

"Listen to understand, not to respond."

–Anonymous

As noted in Chapter 6, fundamental to prospecting is being a good listener. You'll have more success in prospecting to the small- to mid-size market by doing more listening than talking with key people, including the small business owners who make the decisions. True sales opportunities arise from a series of fact-finding or needs-assessment meetings with clients rather than a cookie-cutter "dog and pony show" revealing your capabilities in a "one size fits all" manner. Pay particular attention to two important considerations during the prospecting phase:

1. *Listen to the employer.* Separate yourself from the rest of the competition by being a good listener. Don't go into an initial meeting citing all the reasons why your retirement program is designed to fit all the employer's needs. You need to hear about the company's needs before you can design a solution. As we've mentioned before, it's critical to demonstrate that you can solve the employer's problem, not just sell a product.
2. *Remove obstacles and objections.* By getting the employer's concerns out in the open immediately, you can meet objections

FIGURE 8.1 *Life Cycle of an Employer-Sponsored Retirement Plan Sale*

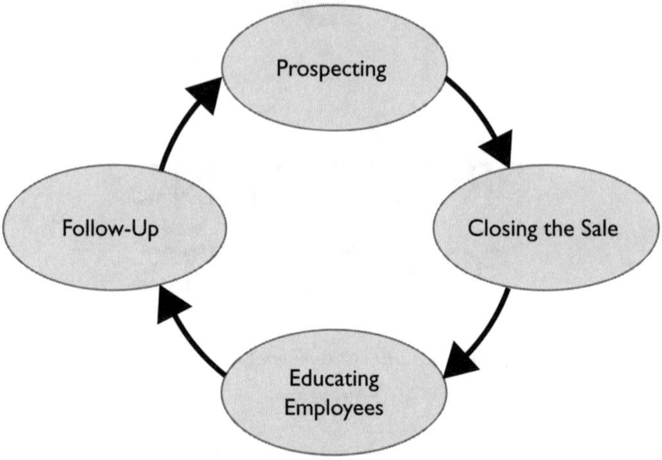

The sales process for employer-sponsored retirement plans isn't a single transaction. Instead, it's a life cycle sale with four key stages of development. At every stage, you have the opportunity to make your mark and differentiate yourself in the eye of the employer. This sales life cycle begins at the prospecting stage. Here, it's vital to be a good listener. A key aspect of closing the sale is showing what makes you different. In the education phase, you build trust and uncover hidden opportunities. The reward for consistent follow-up is client retention, rollover business, and ancillary sales.

that come up. For prospects that currently have plans, you can ask what works and doesn't work for them. For those that don't have plans yet, ask open-ended questions to understand their concerns. As an example, you could ask, "What is the most important thing you want to accomplish with your company's plan?" Chapter 10 presents more detail on this important Solutions Based Selling approach.

PRACTICE MAKES PERFECT

Sales organizations have used a "practice makes perfect" approach for years. They want their salespeople to have instant suc-

Prospecting Corporate Retirement Plans:
Ask Three Magic Questions

When prospecting for employer-sponsored retirement plans, make a
point of always asking your prospect or client these three magic questions:

1. Looking at your current retirement plan, what qualities and features do you like best, and which are most important to you?
2. In your current retirement program, what areas would you like
   to see improved, and where are its weaknesses?
3. If I could show you a program that has _____ (the things you want/
   like), yet at the same time solves _____ (the things you don't like
   about the current plan), is there any reason why you wouldn't
   change plans?

The bottom line: Find out the clients' problems before offering
any solutions.

cess, so they encourage them to sell in an environment where
they've already established confidence and trust.

Whether you're a seasoned salesperson or relatively new, ask
your clients, friends, family, and network if you can make a practice presentation for their retirement plans. If they're not at the
executive level in their company, find out who is and contact those
individuals. You may be surprised at how many of these practice
sessions result in sales! Even if they don't, you'll get to improve
your presentation and avoid costly errors.

Also, look for resources you can tap into through the team that
supports you. For example, does the service provider have an ac-
tuary on staff who can participate in the presentation to an actuar-
ial firm? If so, invite that professional to the presentation. This
person's presence will boost your credibility with your prospect
and build trust and confidence.

We believe that more than half of the sale comes down to trust
and confidence, and this just may be the most difficult piece of clos-

Information to Gather from the Person Who Handles the Plan on a Day-to-Day Basis

1. What investment company is your current plan with?
2. Who is your current third-party administrator (TPA)?
3. What are the plan's approximate total assets?
4. Approximately how much do you send into the plan every year (employee versus employer contributions)?
5. Does your plan have a surrender fee or a contingent deferral sales charge?
6. How many people are eligible to participate in your current plan?
7. How many people actually participate in your current plan?
8. May I have a list of the funds your participants currently have to choose from?
9. May I have a copy of your current fee schedule?
10. Would you or any of your employees like to find a way to put more money into your accounts?
11. What do the employees like best about the plan? What do you like best?
12. What do the employees dislike about the plan? What do you dislike?

The bottom line: Make sure the decision makers and the person who handles the plan on a day-to-day basis are present when you do your finals presentation.

ing new business. So if you've already built trusted relationships within your network of friends and business colleagues, you've just jumped the biggest hurdle. Start with friendly prospects who are members of your target market. Aim for success early on. Build up your confidence to maintain a high level of energy about the retirement plans business and leap over any hurdles you may encounter on your path. Practice helps you accomplish this.

Todd's Story: Practice Presentations Work!

When my daughter took a part-time sales job before starting law school, I was proud and excited that she was following in her father's footsteps. This job was selling vacuum cleaners. (Excuse me, not vacuum cleaners, but "Total Cleaning Systems"—sorry, Ashley.)

As a part of her training, she needed to make 15 practice presentations to friends and family members. Several of those "practice" presentations resulted in sales. Doing these training presentations gave her an opportunity to practice her pitch (plus the chance to make a sale or two). But mostly she benefited by receiving honest feedback from the people closest to her.

Several sales organizations have used this approach for years. They understand that it's important for their salespeople to have instant success.

Consider making practice presentations about corporate retirement plans in an environment where you've already established confidence and trust: current clients, friends, family, and your business network. If your contacts aren't at the executive level in their companies, ask them who is and contact those individuals. You may be surprised at how many of these practice sessions result in sales! And even if they don't result in sales, you'll learn how to improve your presentation and avoid costly errors.

Here's how the conversation to approach a business contact might proceed:

You: "Hi, Bob, how have you been since our last Chamber of Commerce meeting?"

Bob: "Great! How about you?"

You: "Great, thank you. Say, Bob, you know I've been an investment representative for two years now. I've decided to enhance my business by offering corporate retirement plans. Would you be willing to give me constructive criticism by listening to my presentation?"

Bob: "Sure. I'd be happy to. Let's set a time."

Like anything else, finding the most efficient use of your time to approach people produces the greatest return on your investment. Many successful retirement plan salespeople achieve their results in different ways, many of which are shared throughout this book.

Whether you approach your prospects through radio advertising, newspaper advertising, direct-mail campaigns, cold-calling over the telephone or in person, it's completely up to you. But before you find which one of those channels you're most comfortable using, look in your own backyard. If you've been a financial professional for any amount of time, the secret can lie right within your own surroundings. When marketing your corporate retirement plans, consider focusing on clients, friends, and individuals you know through civic organizations. Above all, don't overlook your family members!

As we stated earlier, two elements can represent more than half of the sale: trust and confidence. Gaining a prospect's trust and confidence can be the most difficult part of closing new business. But if you've already built trusting relationships with people you can help, you've already jumped the biggest hurdle. These relationships can present you with your best opportunities for early success, as my daughter discovered. And that can give you the confidence necessary to maintain the energy you'll need to jump the hurdles ahead in the long run.

The bottom line: Conduct practice presentations and take the feedback you receive to heart. Practice can help you build confidence and win business among people in your target market.

THE FIVE MOST COMMON PROSPECTING MISTAKES

What are some of the most common mistakes financial professionals make when selling retirement plans? Take a look at these.

Mistake 1: Wasting time with prospects who offer little chance of success. Some financial professionals chase anyone who breathes and is willing to talk to them. This is a poor use of your time. Let us explain it this way.

What if you were at the end of a presentation with a prospect and met with one of the following responses:

- No, we just moved our plan three months ago. But I've known Joe Financial Professional for years and I'll give Joe my time whenever he needs it.
- We're really not interested in changing at this time. We're very happy with who we're with, but we're always willing to find out if there are better alternatives available.
- Due to our relationship with our financial professional, we would never be interested. (Or, we aren't able to change financial professionals.) But we would be interested in seeing if there is a better product available.

Do your homework, and don't forget about your focus on Solutions Based Selling. Too often, financial professionals spend hours preparing presentations when they actually have limited opportunity to win the business. Don't waste your time. If you've followed a Solutions Based Selling approach, you'll never waste your time, because you'll always be presenting solutions and opportunities for employers to improve their plans.

Mistake 2: Not showing the financial professional's value. Some financial professionals think it's all about cost, investment options, or both. They fail to realize that they've turned the sales process into a commodity instead of a process. They've accidentally eliminated any reason for clients to assume that all products aren't created equally. In fact, in the eyes of the decision maker, these salespeople may have eliminated the need for a financial professional by suggesting that no value can be found outside of cost and investment performance. In reality, the financial professional offers value throughout the process, including helping employers select the right solution to meet their needs, offering guidance regarding fiduciary responsibility, presenting the plan to employees at the initial enrollment meeting, and holding annual reviews for plan participants. If cost is an issue when presenting to clients, you can present different types of plans. Again, keep the focus on Solutions Based Selling. You're there to provide answers to problems, not to sell products per se.

Mistake 3: Rolling out a product "solution" before hearing the client's needs. Too often, financial professionals will go in with both guns blazing. They're on a mission to tell prospects what they should do, what they should buy, and when they should make the decision. Meanwhile, clients patiently (or impatiently) listen to presentations about topics that aren't important to them. They sit back and say, "This isn't the solution we're looking for." The professional has presented his own agenda without providing solutions for the prospects' agendas.

Mistake 4: Presenting a spreadsheet "buffet" of products instead of focusing on solutions. The financial professional brings in a spreadsheet showing how a few different service providers stack up against each other. Again, this turns the sale process into a presentation on commodities—not valued-added solutions. To display a variety of different providers, you'd need pages of categories. Unfortunately, most financial professionals only show the four or five categories they believe are most important. This isn't providing a service to the clients; it's actually a disservice to them.

Mistake 5: Treating this like a "run and done" business. The professional wins the initial sale but loses all of the ancillary sales. The professional makes initial efforts once a sale has been made, then fails to provide the ongoing service and attention that

---

*Todd's Story: What Can Happen When an Employee
Gets Excited about a Plan*

A few years ago, a financial professional invited me to make a presentation with him. He told me that after meeting with me, he asked each of his clients to bring in their corporate retirement plan statements the next time he reviewed their account. One of these clients worked in a manufacturing company. He worked out on the line, with no supervisory power, let alone any decision-making power on the retirement plan.

When the financial professional reviewed this employee's account, he noticed that the asset allocation the employee was using was inappropriate. He also knew the investments within the plan were mediocre at best. The professional discovered that this employee had been given very little education through the employer and didn't really understand his statements, so he provided suggestions on how to better allocate his funds.

Next, the professional pulled out a quarterly statement from a different provider and showed it to the employee. The employee felt the alternative statement was easier to understand and provided better information than his current statement.

Then the professional pulled out a list of funds available through his service provider and compared those with the client to the ones he had to choose from in his existing 401(k). He asked, "Wouldn't you like to have a statement like this and funds with performance like these?" The employee responded with an enthusiastic yes.

Then the professional showed him the provider's Web site, and the employee was amazed by how easy its navigation was. The professional then asked, "Wouldn't you like to have a Web site like this?" The employee excitedly responded with another yes. Next, the professional asked, "Who is in charge of your corporate retirement plan?" "The company's CFO," was the reply. He asked if he could initiate contact with the CFO using the employee as a referral source. Another yes.

Unfortunately when the professional contacted the CFO, she wasn't as interested in the idea of changing the corporate retirement plan as the employee was. But within two weeks, the same CFO called the professional. She said that, while she still wasn't interested in looking at alternative plans, this employee had told several employees about "the new 401(k) plan" the company was going to adopt, how great the statements and the Web site were, and how impressive the investment selection was. This spurred other employees to get excited and ask the CFO when the new plan was taking effect. Now she had a predicament. Enough employees had indicated an interest in looking at different retirement plans that she felt she needed to see what all the excitement was over. She invited the professional to make a presentation to her and the company president. They accepted his proposal and within weeks, the professional had more than $1,000,000 in assets and 30 new employees to prospect for ancillary assets.

The bottom line: A prospect doesn't need to be the decision maker. The prospect can be someone who works on the manufacturing line or anywhere else in the company.

employer-sponsored retirement plans require. Eventually this financial professional will lose the plan to someone else. Worse yet, the professional never fully realizes the enormous opportunities he or she could have found through ancillary assets and sales.

Never overlook or underestimate connections with employees in your prospective organizations who aren't the final decision makers. You can communicate with the people who have access to decision makers as well as with the decision makers themselves.

Here's what often happens: You get an audience with the decision makers and present a proposal that they acknowledge is impressive and would work well for their company. But right now, they say, they've got a lot of hot irons in the fire and they need to put the retirement plan on the "back burner." While we believe they have the best of intentions, the program they were once excited about has now gathered dust and they have forgotten the passionate presentation you delivered. But had we made the presentation in front of both the key decision maker *and* the person who administrates the plan day to day, we may have been able to keep the retirement plan a "front burner" topic by exposing issues the decision maker may not have been aware of but the administrative person is. That could further ignite a sense of urgency because it lights up that person like a Christmas tree by providing the solutions to the needs he or she has identified.

More than just being persistent, gatekeepers shed light on the problems and complaints from which decision makers are insulated in their daily work life. Hearing about problems they didn't know existed can place your proposal higher on their priority lists. That's why it's critical to nurture alliances among the people in the retirement area. You show them a workable process; they get excited about it, and they share that excitement with the decision makers.

We see this often with our own Retirement Plans Group at The Hartford. We'll spend a great deal of time educating the sales support professionals at a firm we do business with on our retirement plans story and the opportunity for financial professionals. If we do a good job telling the story again and again, this positive message almost always filters up to senior management and out to financial professionals at the firm.

TRY THIS COLD-CALLING APPROACH

When cold-calling in person, we would suggest that you keep it simple. Get a prospect report from your provider of choice. When you walk in the door, you should know exactly whom you need to ask for. Here's how the dialog might go:

> Receptionist: "Hello, may I help you?"
> Professional: "Hello! My name is John Smith." Hand the receptionist one of your business cards. "I am here to see Ms. Decision Maker. But first, may I have your permission to tell you three things?"
> Receptionist: "Sure."
> Professional: "I have to apologize because I don't have an appointment with Ms. Decision Maker. I'm only looking for five minutes of her time. I'm not here to talk about gaining her personal investment business."

A conversation like this could get you escorted out the door quickly, because a company may be strict on only taking people by appointment. However, you might actually interest a decision maker because you were kind enough to apologize first and ask for only five minutes, while confirming that you're not soliciting their personal business.

WHAT TO ASK IN YOUR INITIAL INTERVIEW WITH THE DECISION MAKER

Keep your initial interview with the decision maker simple and brief. The key to efficiency lies with the first impression you make and the first questions you ask. Practice using these four magic questions and see what you're able to accomplish.

Question 1: If you were to make a change in your plan, what qualities in your existing plan would you like to maintain in the new plan?

Ask this question to find out what they like about their current program. What features do they value, what is important to them, and why? What are their hot buttons? What features about the proposed program will they find valuable?

Question 2: Assuming you did change your current plan, what areas would you like to see improved?

As with the first question, it's important to find out the reasons behind the answers they're giving. Once the question has been asked but before moving on to the next question, repeat back to the decision maker what you *think* you heard. You want to make sure that the communication has been properly received.

Question 3: What concerns do you have about potentially changing plans?

It is important to recognize and understand that, while employers may want to make a change, they may have been burned by previous bad experiences. Be alert to learning about issues that, whether they're real or perceived, you can address. Look for indicators that your prospects feel comfortable before going to the next level in this Solutions Based Selling process.

Question 4: If I could show you an alternative program that _____ (list all the features the person brought up in question #1) and provide a better _____ (solutions to question #2), yet you felt comfortable beyond any doubt that _____ (solutions to question #3) could be maintained, would you change plans?

It's a blunt question that needs to be asked—would you change plans? Too many financial professionals have gone through long, drawn-out processes only to find out that the employer is deeply committed to the current plan provider. Or, while they may consider changing plans, they have no intention of changing financial professionals. Find out why from the start. Get a commitment that they're interested up front (or at least understand their objection and its roots), or cut your losses and leave. If you get decision makers to commit to a sale, as long as you do what you say you can do, then you've gained a committed prospect in five minutes or less. If they say no, then find out why they feel this way. That's why asking decision makers why they wouldn't switch is critical. If the answer is that the company's financial professional of record is the owner's brother-in-law, you'd be wise to look for another prospect. To suggest acting in the best interest of plan participants over maintaining family relations is usually ill advised.

Often, the objections will be valid in a prospect's mind but not valid in the real world. In these situations, your role is to put the prospect's mind at ease. Here's an example of how you could accomplish this:

> Prospect: "I wouldn't be interested in moving my plan, given the market's current condition (up or down)."
>
> You: "If I could prove to you beyond any doubt in your mind that regardless of where the market is at (or going) you should consider making a change, would you consider changing plans?"
>
> Prospect: "But we just changed plans three years ago!"
>
> You: "While I understand that you have changed plans within the last three years, if I could prove to you beyond any doubt that there are sufficient reasons to make a change, is there any reason why you wouldn't change plans?"

The point is clear: find out the underlying objections, rational or not, as soon as you can.

USING THE EMPLOYER 401(k) FACT FINDER

Here is an example of a fact-finding tool used by The Hartford in the prospecting stages.

Please complete the following for each prospect:

Company name: _____

Address: _____

Phone/fax/e-mail: _____

Your contact: _____ Decision maker: _____

Type of Business:

❑ Corporation ❑ Subchapter-S ❑ Partnership ❑ Nonprofit ❑ Governmental

❑ Other: _____

Is this business affiliated with any other business? ❑ No ❑ Yes: _____

Total number of employees: _____ % full-time: _____ % part-time: _____

Currently have a 401(k) plan? ❑ No (complete section below)
❑ Yes (complete section on reverse side)

New Plan Prospects:

Please rate the following 401(k) program benefits according to importance. Using a scale of 1 (least important) to 5 (most important), circle one:

1 2 3 4 5   Keep benefit costs low and predictable?

1 2 3 4 5   Attract and retain quality employees?

1 2 3 4 5   Provide employees with an opportunity to save for their retirement on a tax-deferred basis?

1 2 3 4 5   Provide yourself with an opportunity to save for your retirement on a tax-deferred basis?

1 2 3 4 5   Take advantage of additional corporate tax deductions?

Please rate the following 401(k) program features according to importance. Using a scale of 1 (least important) to 5 (most important), circle one:

1 2 3 4 5   Investment diversity

1 2 3 4 5   Investment performance

1 2 3 4 5   Reasonable cost/fees

1 2 3 4 5   Plan design flexibility

1 2 3 4 5   Participant education materials

1 2 3 4 5   Participant services (VRU, Internet, etc.)

If interested in starting a 401(k) program, when would you like to start one? _____

Why haven't you already set up a 401(k) plan? ❑ Too expensive ❑ Too complex

❑ Not enough interest ❑ Other _____

Please complete the following for each prospect:

Are you completely satisfied with your
plan? If not, why? _____

Have key/highly-compensated employees
been restricted from time to time in the
amount of money they are able to contribute?   ❑ Yes   ❑ No

Have key/highly-compensated employees
had their pretax contributions returned
after the year due to not meeting plan
testing requirements?   ❑ Yes   ❑ No

Does your plan limit employee contributions
to some stated percentage of pay
(example: 15% or 20%)?   ❑ Yes   ❑ No

If possible, would key employees be interested
in discussing ways to maximize their annual
contributions?   ❑ Yes   ❑ No

What are your plan's current assets? _____

What are your ongoing contributions
per month to the plan? _____

Does your plan have a surrender charge?   ❑ No   ❑ Yes, amount: _____

Do you have tool(s) and/or a process in place
that provides for an ongoing evaluation and
analysis of your investment choices?   ❑ Yes   ❑ No

How do you feel about the investments'
performance?   ❑ Above expectations   ❑ As expected   ❑ Below expectations

Are you satisfied with the number of
investment categories?   ❑ Yes   ❑ No: (circle one)   Too few   Too many

Are you satisfied with the number of
investment choices?   ❑ Yes   ❑ No: (circle one)   Too few   Too many

What do you consider most important
when selecting investment choices?   ❑ Low fees   ❑ Well-known money manager(s)   ❑ Diversification/Quantity

How do you feel about your provider's
service and your plan's administrative support?   ❑ Above expectations   ❑ As expected   ❑ Below expectations

    If "below expectations," please comment: _____

Is your current provider responsive to
your issues/concerns?   ❑ Yes   ❑ No

Do you have a dedicated service account
representative for your plan?   ❑ Yes   ❑ No

Do you currently send data/contributions
electronically?   ❑ Yes   ❑ No

What level of investment knowledge
do your participants have?   ❑ Beginner   ❑ Intermediate   ❑ Advanced

What is your plan participation rate? _____

    Are you satisfied with this participation?   ❑ Yes   ❑ No

Do your participants receive quarterly
statements sent to their homes?   ❑ Yes   ❑ No

Do your participants have the ability to
enroll into the plan via the Internet?   ❑ Yes   ❑ No

Does your provider conduct regular
on-site enrollment/re-enrollment meetings?   ❑ Yes   ❑ No

How much is your annual recordkeeping fee? _____

How much is your annual participant fee? _____

Are there any extra fees?   ❑ No   ❑ Yes for: _____

Do you believe you are paying a fair price
for the value of the actual services and
benefits you receive?   ❑ Yes   ❑ No

Getting an Education in Cold-Calling

Many professionals hire a staff person to do cold-calling. If you live in a community where there is a business college, you could tap into the availability and eagerness of students at that college. Bring in one or two interns and work out a script for them to use when calling prospects for your practice. Many business owners enjoy helping students and are willing to answer questions.

As you write the questions, though, make sure they don't cross over into questions that only licensed professionals are allowed to ask. Check with your firm's compliance department about the wording of these questions.

The bottom line: Business students and others in your community may be qualified and eager to help you with cold calls. Tap into that resource.

THREE CHARACTERISTICS OF A GOOD PROSPECT

In a majority of situations, you can determine if certain employers are good prospects if one or more of these characteristics are present: pain, fear, and greed. Let's look at each of these more closely.

Pain. If you've spent time in a health club, you've heard the saying "no pain, no gain." In many instances, that couldn't be truer than in employer-sponsored retirement plan sales. Instead of pushing a product onto a client, you want to find solutions to the pain a client is currently experiencing. Sources of pain could be excessively high fees, employees not getting the education to make informed decisions, no fiduciary support, or unacceptable plan administration. A company can be experiencing pain for a multitude of reasons. It's your obligation to find out why and propose solutions to eliminate it.

Fear. One of the largest concerns today is employers' required fiduciary responsibility and liability within the corporate retirement plan. In our litigious society, lawsuits related to corporate retirement plans are pushing their way to the top of the list of fears. If you can recognize and communicate an understanding of fiduciary responsibility and liability, you can earn decision makers' trust and confidence.

Greed. If you can show employers a way to reduce costs and accumulate money—whether for their participants, for highly compensated employees, or for themselves—you may earn their loyalty. Sometimes a better education and support program can be persuasive. Other times, improved plan design or other factors may appeal to employers.

Regardless, it's important to identify which of these emotional triggers they have, why they have them, and what you can do to "pull the trigger" and get the sale. As you learn more about Solutions Based Selling, pay attention to how you build trust and confidence with employers as well as what sets you apart from other financial professionals.

Questions to Move Your Prospects toward Solutions

After you've read this book, created your team, and started to call on prospects, use this section to guide you through the initial prospecting stages. When you call a prospective employer, ask to speak with the human resources manager or benefits administrator. Begin building a relationship by asking the following questions:

- What type of retirement plan do you have for your employees?
- Is your retirement plan up to date?
- Would you like to set an appointment to determine if your plan is current and to determine what steps you need to take to make sure it complies with current laws?

Prospects may indicate that their companies' plans are out of date or they may seem uncertain whether their plans comply with current laws. These responses open doors to move to the next level in your prospecting conversations. Remember, at this point in the sales process, you should have received training and education from the service provider you'll represent. As a result, you'll better understand the terminology—and implications—of the prospecting questions that follow.

If the employer has a 401(k) plan, you can ask these questions:

- Are you aware of recent regulatory changes to your 401(k) plan? Would you like to set up an appointment to review these changes, and I'll show you how to implement them in your plan?
- Have you ever failed your discrimination test and had to return money to your highly compensated employees? Would you like to set up an appointment, and I can show you how to avoid compliance testing problems in the future?
- Are you concerned about potential fiduciary liability under section 404(c) of ERISA? Would you like to set up an appointment so I can show you a way to help reduce your fiduciary liability going forward?

If the employer has a money purchase plan, you can ask these questions:

- Are you aware that you no longer need to make a committed contribution to your money purchase plan to maximize your 25 percent deduction?
- Would you like to set up an appointment to review a flexible alternative with the same deduction limit?
- Would you like to see how you can convert your existing plan to this flexible alternative?

If the employer has a money purchase plan and profit-sharing plan, you can ask these questions:

- Are you aware that you no longer need both a money purchase and a profit-sharing plan to maximize your 25 percent deduction?
- Would you like to set up an appointment to review a way to eliminate the committed obligation in the money purchase plan and hear about a flexible alternative?

If the employer has a profit-sharing plan, you can ask this question:

- Would you like to set up an appointment and allow me to show you a plan that will let you contribute the same amount you are currently contributing, or even less? This will allow the highly compensated individuals in your company to have more money contributed on their behalf and not be deemed discriminatory.

The bottom line: Prepare various questions for the variety of situations you'll find when you begin prospecting.

9

GETTING READY FOR YOUR FINALS PRESENTATION— SERIOUS PREPARATION WILL CARRY THE DAY

"In this business, above all else, there is absolutely no substitute for hard work."

–John Walters, President, U.S. Wealth Management Group, Hartford Life

Some people say you should know your prospects. We disagree. More than knowing your prospects, you need to understand them. Specifically, you need to understand what's motivating their change to a new retirement plan. Learn everything you can about the employers (the potential plan sponsor) so you can put yourself in the best position to win their business.

In particular, be sure to understand these issues as you prepare for your finals presentation:

- What are this client's emotional triggers? What do they represent? For example, is this client feeling the pain of having an out-of-date plan? Might the client make a hasty decision to select the next retirement plan?
- Are you the only professional and provider invited to present a finals presentation? Will others be present? If so, how many others? Who will they be?

- With whom will you be meeting? Decision makers or gate-keepers? A group or an individual? What are their backgrounds? What is their time line to make a change?
- Most important, why is this company making a change?

This chapter outlines the critical steps needed to prepare for your finals presentation. Keep in mind that these steps are an extension of the Solutions Based Selling approach. Start by understanding everything you can about your client. Doing so puts you in the best position to provide an individualized, on-target solution, gain the client's trust and confidence, and win the sale.

HOW TO USE THE OPPORTUNITY DIAGNOSTIC WORKSHEET

How do you know if you're in a good position to win the business? You may have a strong gut feeling, but beware—even highly experienced salespeople can be misled by their emotions.

At The Hartford, we use a measurement tool based on research information from a variety of plans we've won—and lost. The Opportunity Diagnostic Worksheet identifies six key areas that affect the client's buying decision. As we prepare to meet with a client, we go through this worksheet to know whether we're in a position to win. The objective results give us insight about:

- How to approach this client
- Whether we're ready for the finals presentation
- How to ask for and win the business

Why do we use a diagnostic tool? Why not simply listen to our intuition? In a word: *objectivity*. As an example, one of The Hartford's retirement plans specialists we'll call Stacy was absolutely convinced the company would win a certain client's retirement plan business. Todd held several conference calls with both the financial professional involved and Stacy, yet he wasn't convinced that The

Hartford would win the business. During a phone conversation with Stacy, Todd began asking questions from the diagnostics worksheet, weaving them into the conversation. Unfortunately, every answer that Stacy gave was a negative one, indicating The Hartford wasn't poised to win this client's business. After the third set of questions, Stacy realized Todd was using the diagnostic worksheet. Todd admitted that he was and asked, "Do you understand why?" With that, Stacy realized she had been letting her emotions get in the way of seeing the situation objectively. Using this tool is a great way to step back and analyze the situation with clarity.

Remember, when you walk in the door you may only have one shot to win the business. This diagnostic tool helps you know whether you're ready to go in or whether you need to do more homework. Figure 9.1 shows The Hartford's Opportunity Diagnostic Worksheet. Use the larger version of this worksheet, which can be found in Appendix 5, for your prospecting activities.

Let's take a closer look at the Opportunity Diagnostic Worksheet's six key areas.

Key area 1: Opportunity qualification—How well qualified is this opportunity? Is the client open to making a change from the current retirement plan provider? How often does this company review its retirement plan? Does your service provider already provide other products and services to your prospective plan sponsor? Do you have access to senior people to make a presentation?

Key area 2: Competitive situation—What is the competitive landscape? Are you the only presenter, competing against the incumbent? Or are other providers vying for this business as well? If so, how many providers? Do you understand your competitors' selling strategies? Do you have a thorough game plan to go after this opportunity tactically and strategically?

Key area 3: Customer knowledge—What is your depth of understanding about this company? What are this company's strategies, objectives, key products, and challenges, and how does

FIGURE 9.1 *The Hartford's Opportunity Diagnostic Worksheet*

Opportunity Diagnostic Worksheet

1) Opportunity Qualification (0 to 17 Points)	Point Value	2) Competitive Situation (-5 to 5 Points)	Point Value
Measurement Criteria:		Measurement Criteria:	
☐ The plan sponsor is open to making a change.		☐ A competitive broker (or vendor) has a small share of the customer's business.	
☐ We know when they will review their 401k plan.		☐ A competitive broker (or vendor) has their own supporters in the account.	
☐ Hartford Life is already providing product/services to the business.		☐ We fully understand the competitive broker's (or vendor's) selling strategy.	
☐ We have access to the senior decision maker to make a presentation.		☐ We have developed a plan to secure this account.	
Total Score:		Total Score:	

3) Customer Knowledge (0 to 13 Points)	Point Value	4) Strength of Support (0 to 35 Points)	Point Value
Measurement Criteria:		Measurement Criteria:	
☐ We understand the department(s) within the company that our solution impacts. For example, we know the department's objectives, strategies, key projects, and challenges.		☐ We have identified one or more key players in the company to align with.	
☐ We know the customer's principle line of business.		☐ We have access to contacts who are open to sharing information.	
☐ We know their target market, their competition, and how they differentiate themselves from their competitors.		☐ We have built relationships with contacts who will give us information they wouldn't give the competitor.	
☐ We know their key objectives and the strategies they will implement to achieve these objectives.		☐ We have contacts who believe our product or service is superior to the competition's and are willing to assist us (i.e., a champion).	
☐ We know the challenges facing them in their marketplace.		☐ We have a contact who wants you to win because of their strong relationship with you.	
☐ We know key business issues from your/our discussions with your contacts.		☐ We have more than one supporter/champion/coach.	
Total Score:		Total Score:	

5) Impact of Detractors (-25 to 0 Points)	Point Value	6) Decision-Making Process (0 to 27 Points)	Point Value
Measurement Criteria:		Measurement Criteria:	
☐ We have identified a contact in the account that is aligned with a competitive broker (or vendor).		☐ We know who made the previous decision.	
☐ We have contacts who have verbalized their belief that the competitor's product is superior.		☐ We know who will have influence on the decision.	
☐ We have contacts who want us to lose and are blocking our selling strategy.		☐ We know who truly owns the decision.	
☐ Your contact forces us to work through them and restricts access to other people.		☐ We know the difference between who will be "making the recommendation" versus who will be making the decision.	
Total Score:		Total Score:	

Summary	Score
1) Opportunity Qualification (0 to 17 Points)	
2) Competitive Situation (-5 to 5 Points)	
3) Customer Knowledge (0 to 13 Points)	
4) Strength of Support (0 to 35 Points)	
5) Impact of Detractor (-25 to 0 Points)	
6) Decision-Making Process (0 to 27 Points)	
Total:	

a retirement plan fit into that? Do you understand this company's principal line of business? Its target market? Do you know its key future strategies and objectives and how the company plans to implement them? What challenges does this company face in the marketplace? What are its employee demographics? Do you know the company's competition and its competitive differentiators?

Knowing these factors helps you understand the psychology of this buyer. If you use the same approach with your audience that they use with their target market, they'll relate to you. For example, during the presentation, you can cite exactly how their products stand out from their competition's, then tie that into how you and your service provider stand out from your competition. This helps your clients make the decision to "go with themselves" and buy from you. Match your presentation with how they think. When in Rome, be a Roman.

Of course, learn all you can about the company's current retirement plan, if it has one, and what the decision makers are seeking in a new retirement plan. Before your presentation ask: Is there an investor policy statement? Does the company's day-to-day administrator hear complaints or compliments from plan participants? What is the current investment allocation? (You can tell a lot about how well employees are educated and how well the professional is doing. For example, if employees are chasing performance, this is a sign that they haven't been serviced—employees aren't receiving sufficient education to make informed decisions.) Do they have a proper filing system? (You might bring an example of a proper filing system and explain its importance. Show a sample during your presentation and tell your prospective clients that it's one of the areas in which you'll coach them.)

Key area 4: Strength of support—How much support do we have within this organization? Have you identified one or more key players? Do you have an inside champion fighting your battles with you? Do you have access to inside contacts who are open to sharing information with you—both before the presentation, to warn about any challenges you'll face, and after the presentation, to give feedback on what you did right and wrong? Better yet, through initial phases of this process, can you build a relationship with someone in the organization who will share information with you but not a competitor? Do you have a true champion within the company who believes your product is superior to your competitors' products and is willing to assist you? For example, perhaps the chief financial officer had a positive experience with your service provider at her previous company or personally has investments with your service provider.

Key area 5: Impact of detractors—What is the possible effect from people in the company who don't support you? Don't skip over this critical point. You must identify anyone at the company who is aligned with your competition, either a competitive financial professional or service provider. Have people told you they believe a competitor's product is superior? Carefully watch out for this deadly landmine: Does someone in the organization—whether a decision maker or not—want you to lose the business? Is this individual actively blocking your selling strategy? Understand what forces are at play, both working in your direction and working against you.

Key area 6: Decision-making process—Do you have a handle on all aspects of this process? It's important to learn who selected the company's previous (current) provider. Why did this person select that financial professional and service provider? Be careful! You don't want to offend that person, even if he is unhappy with the current provider. Identify who will have any influence on this buying decision. Sometimes the decision maker is one person: the president, CEO, and 100 percent owner of the company. Yet the day-to-day administrator may actually drive the decision, having the true influence, even though the decision maker signs the paperwork.

The person who drives the decision is as important as the decision maker. If multiple parties attend your presentation, make sure you understand who'll make recommendations versus who'll make the final decision and actually sign on the dotted line. Don't try to close with the wrong person! You could block yourself out of a sale by getting assertive with the wrong individual.

Does the decision maker have a team of professionals? Sometimes the business owner or key players have a "value group" of attorneys or CPAs they turn to for consultation and direction. Of your competitors, few will ask if the decision makers have confidants to whom they turn for business reasons. Take time to meet with these confidants and sell to them as well. By doing so, you'll double your odds of winning by gaining their confidence and trust.

Dig deep. Learn as much as you can about the plan design the company *really* wants. What components are most important to this client? Why does this company currently have a retirement plan? Does this company want to create an employee benefit primarily designed to help its employees, or are there additional motivations such as a tax shelter for highly compensated employees and company officers? Will the new plan have overweighted contributions to a select group of individuals? Look at the previous years' compliance testing information. Does this company have participation problems or other testing problems? Be sure to identify them.

PREPARE YOUR PITCH—THEN REHEARSE, REHEARSE, REHEARSE

You've done your homework, and the diagnostics test indicates that, yes, you're ready to approach this client. Now invest the necessary time to prepare your presentation. Rehearse it until you know it thoroughly. Don't rush through this step. Does this sound like too much work? Remember: this step may be the difference between the average salesperson, who may close 30 percent of business opportunities, and stellar performers like Michael (whom we introduced in the Introduction) who close 65 percent of their business opportunities.

Michael takes the time to see the presentation through the eyes of his clients. He asks himself, "If I were sitting in their chairs, walking in their shoes, what would I want to know?" He makes it easy to understand his pitch by tying it into what he knows about the company as well as the individuals he'll meet.

Michael may know that four other agent/provider teams are coming to the table, representing dozens of fund families. They all have user-friendly Web sites and tout great service. He looks for other ways to be different by investing the time to understand this client's exact situation. He prepares his presentation, rehearses it, tweaks it, and rehearses more. His presentation is much more polished and on target than his competitors' presentations. As he strikes a personable chord with the clients, he's in a good position to win their business.

The next chapter offers tips and techniques to make targeted, memorable presentations and close the business. As you can see, the Solution Based Selling process combines specific techniques, research, and a powerful sales approach to put you in the best position to win the sale.

10

TACTICS AND STRATEGIES FOR PRESENTING WELL AND CLOSING THE SALE

"Imagination is more important than knowledge."

–Albert Einstein

You've done your homework, set an appointment to give your finals presentation to a prospective client, and confirmed that the decision maker will attend this meeting. You're nearly ready to make your finals presentation.

At this stage, review the following checklist to ensure you're ready:

- Did you complete the Opportunity Diagnostics Worksheet (see Appendix 5)? Do you need to address any issues raised in the worksheet's six sections?
- Have you prepared and rehearsed your presentation?
- Do you have visual aids such as educational guides in addition to your presentation?
- Have you created a written agenda to hand out?
- Have you prepared your introduction so you can introduce your team and clearly explain everyone's roles?

Now you're ready to present your finals presentation to your client. The following tactics and strategies dovetail to provide the crescendo moment—closing the deal.

PRESENTATION TACTICS: SET THE STAGE FOR SUCCESS

Some surprisingly straightforward tactics will help you lay the foundation for a successful finals presentation. Remember, you're setting the stage to ask for the business, get the client to say yes, and close the deal. Here are eight key tactics that will get you the business.

Tactic 1: At the beginning of the meeting, confirm how much time you'll have. Often, we'll call and confirm with clients to ensure that we'll have 1½ hours for our finals presentation. Even if we confirm that morning, sometimes when we arrive in the afternoon, we learn that something has come up for the client. All of a sudden, we may only have 45 minutes instead of 90 minutes. Other times, we discover that we have more time available for our presentation than we'd planned.

It's important to establish the allotted time up front. If you don't have this brief conversation at the beginning of the meeting and you actually have less time than you thought, you can tell when you hit the clients' time limit. They lose focus, quit listening, and start fidgeting. As soon as you notice these body signals, wrap up your presentation. Unfortunately, you may not have presented the most crucial areas of content. If you confirm the available time at the beginning of the meeting, you can shorten your presentation and focus on the most important areas.

Tactic 2: Ask clients what they want to accomplish in the time available. This question can reveal surprising information. You may discover that their objective is to move forward immediately; they're ready to sign the paperwork, thanks to your initial conversations and relationship building. In this case, if you had proceeded with your presentation, you could have damaged your chances by overselling.

Plan to be flexible! Even though you've spent a great deal of time preparing and rehearsing, you need to be prepared if you find out that their objectives vary from what you'd determined or the biggest emotional trigger isn't what you thought it would be. Be prepared to change direction on the fly.

Tactic 3: Review the agenda with your clients. Once you understand your clients' time constraints and their objectives for the meeting, hand out copies of the agenda you prepared, walk through the items you propose to cover in the available time, and explain why you think it's important to talk about each item on the agenda. Change the agenda as necessary to address topics that are of utmost concern to the client, and cross out items that aren't critical.

Tactic 4: Summarize previous conversations and activities. What has brought everyone to this point? With whom have you met? What information did you discover in your due diligence that is worth sharing? Briefly summarize the relevant points so the decision maker is brought up to date and can quickly gain understanding of the activities and discussions going on behind the scenes.

Tactic 5: Introduce your team. Explain the roles of each person on the team and the part each one will play if you have the honor of winning the client's business. Also, ask your audience members to introduce themselves and explain their roles. Usually the business owner/CEO, human resources director, and benefits administrator or payroll supervisor attend the finals presentations.

Tactic 6: Present your topics in the order of the agenda. Keep in mind that it's important to create solid relationships using the Solutions Based Selling approach. And remember, the key isn't *knowing* your clients as much as *understanding* them. If you've taken time in previous meetings to educate your clients, you should have a handle on what's important to them. Ask "Which topic on the agenda would you like to talk about first?" They may look at your agenda and go for the first item on your list.

Their choice tells you a great deal. First, it indicates that you read the situation right—you identified the topic that's most important to these clients. Second, having clients answer this question puts them in control. Instead of attending a presentation and being "talked to," they're involved in selecting the discussion topics. This approach helps create a level playing field and gets them actively working to solve their problem. The meeting becomes less of a presentation and more of a brainstorming session.

Tactic 7: Take a "time pulse" ten minutes before the meeting ends. Move through your presentation, following the agenda. Be conscious and respectful of the time allotted. If you're running out of time, stop about five minutes before the meeting is scheduled to end and say, "Listen, we said we had 45 minutes. We're at 40 minutes with 5 minutes left. What would you like to do with the last 5 minutes? What do you want to cover?" Your clients will tell you what they really want to find out about. They may even extend the meeting time, which is great. Take this as a buying signal.

Tactic 8: Keep all audience members engaged. Throughout the presentation, it's critical to remain engaged in the discussion. It's even more important to keep the clients in your audience involved in the entire discussion. If more than five or ten minutes pass without your clients actively participating, the meeting becomes a straight-out presentation instead of a brainstorming session. If listeners lose interest, you risk losing the deal.

WHAT MAKES YOU DIFFERENT FROM YOUR COMPETITORS?

Face it, you'll always have competition. Nearly every employer looking for a new retirement plan reviews plans from at least two financial

Stand Out from the Crowd of Competitors

Remember, winning the client's business isn't about selling a product; it's about approaching the presentation differently. You need to create the one and only presentation that they'll remember and refer to by saying, "That one was different."

Here are some pointers to help you stand out from the competition:

- *Smile.* Smiling is contagious and helps keep the meeting from becoming too serious.
- *Demonstrate passion.* Use a lot of heart in your presentation. Clients will grab onto this, and it'll make a difference.
- *Use visual aids.* These can include video clips, a PowerPoint presentation, or a tour of the service provider's facility.
- *Use silly props.* Reach into a bag, pull out a light bulb, and say, "I have an idea." Or tuck a dollar bill into your shirt pocket before the meeting; pull out the dollar bill and say, "Here, you can pass the buck." These little gags may be corny, but clients laugh—and they help make your presentation fun and memorable.

The bottom line: Make sure your presentation is fun and delivered with passion. Keep clients engaged. Create a presentation that's different from the norm so you and your message will be remembered long after you leave.

professionals. Often, you're competing against multiple financial professionals and providers who will also make finals presentations.

You can assume that you and your competitors will do your homework on a given prospect. You want to know everything there is to know about this client: the employee demographics, products and services, key decision makers, revenue, new business wins, upcoming business opportunities, and more. You and your competitors will likely find most of these facts from the company's Web site. And you'll learn more by using good old-fashioned legwork to research and discover less obvious information that tells you what makes this company tick.

Ask for Permission to Take Notes

At the beginning of the finals presentations, take a moment to ask your clients for permission to take notes. This visual cue shows clients that you truly care and respect them. Clients never say no to this request. In fact, they appreciate the fact that you asked for permission. Remember what Zig Ziglar said: "They don't care how much you know. They want to know how much you care."

Just like you, your competitors probably will present a reasonable product mix for the clients' retirement plan. If your competitors represent reputable providers, you can assume they're coming to the table with viable products (although probably not solutions) to meet a client's needs.

So how do you win the business? What makes you different from your competitors? We believe it boils down to three key strategies:

1. Bringing in your team of experts
2. Presenting your solution in a way that shows how it meets the company's needs
3. Asking for the business—knowing and believing what makes you different, and communicating that with confidence and passion

This section expands on the three strategies and provides suggestions on how to deliver a presentation that will win over prospects as well as guidance to close the sale and turn retirement plan prospects into clients.

STRATEGY 1: BRING IN YOUR TEAM OF EXPERTS

We're big fans of teams. We have countless examples of increased success rates when financial professionals bring their teams of experts to client presentations. Bringing your team makes a powerful statement to clients. If you schedule a client presentation with an employer, think about the impact of bringing in your team of experts from the client's point of view. From the outset, clients know their questions will be answered by knowledgeable professionals. They'll be impressed that your team has traveled to attend this meeting. They'll get the message that their business is important to you and to the provider. They'll clearly see that your services are backed by experts. They'll understand that when they do business with you, they can draw on the expertise of your team—and build on the relationships that begin in that client presentation meeting.

For obvious logistical reasons, be sure to tell your clients that you're bringing in your team of experts. As we noted earlier, make sure you properly identify everyone on your team at the beginning of the meeting. For example, you'd say:

> Michael is a retirement plans specialist for The Hartford, and his role is to answer your detailed questions about specific plans and investments. Susan is a third-party administrator; her role is to help all of us ensure that your plan complies with all laws and regulations. As your financial professional, my primary role is to be your first point of contact for your retirement plan. I'll also help with the initial enrollment meeting, conduct annual reviews for participating employees to help them understand their allocation options, and help the company meet its fiduciary responsibilities.

Be sure to introduce the employers' representatives and understand their roles as well (for example, the CEO, human resources director, and payroll supervisor). It's critical for everyone to understand why each person is in attendance and their individual responsibilities.

Clear introductions at the beginning of your meeting lay important groundwork for your close. At the end of your presentation, before you ask for the sale, take a moment to ask your clients if they have any questions for you, the provider's representative, or the third-party administrator. This helps you get questions on the table, address all concerns, and determine if your solution meets their needs.

STRATEGY 2: PRESENT SOLUTIONS TO SHOW HOW THEY MEET CLIENTS' NEEDS

You've worked hard to get the background information on the employer and design an individualized plan that covers the clients' needs—as you know them. Now you'll use Solutions Based Selling to identify all their needs even more clearly and show how your solution meets their needs 100 percent. Take note: This approach helps set you up for a powerful closing.

Try the following technique if you're presenting to two or more people. Let's say you're meeting with the CEO, human resources director, and payroll supervisor. Each person has different ideas about what should be included in the company's new retirement plan. Start with a blank piece of paper or a flip chart. Then ask the CEO, "What would you like to see in the ultimate design of this plan? Forget about regulations and laws right now—what serves your needs as CEO of this company?" Write down the answers on the paper or flip chart. Go around the room and write down each point. Notice that you're creating a working document right before their eyes. Your audience is already seeing how your presentation is different from those of your competitors. You'll approach their needs with a solution, not a packaged set of products.

Listen to them—what do they want? Don't do all the talking! Next, ask the human resources representative about his concerns. He might say, "When something goes wrong, the employees call me. I have to deal with myriad issues. So 'ease of administration' is my overall concern." Write this down.

Next, ask the payroll supervisor, "What's important to you?"

"We need to have a seamless transition between our payroll system and the administration of any new plan we select."

Write down this answer. If you anticipate that one of their concerns is investments but this isn't evident in their questions, ask them, "Are you satisfied with the investment performance of your current plan?" Do you see how you're drawing a complete picture of their needs?

Many salespeople come in with a "final" PowerPoint presentation—all set to address certain issues in a certain order. If you know your material, you can move through your presentation in any order to address your audience's top concerns first. The key is knowing your material inside and out. You must feel confident about the information you present and the presentation itself.

Be flexible! Adapt your presentation to show how the solution you propose meets every single need on the list you just created together. If cost is your audience's main concern, skip directly to the cost section in your presentation. Address this issue, then ask your clients if they have any questions about this topic. This sales approach visually reinforces how, point by point, you're addressing each of their needs with a complete solution.

Now ask your audience this question: "Can you think of any other issues affecting cost that I haven't addressed?" Make a point of asking each person in the room, not just the CEO. Flesh out all of their cost concerns. For example, the payroll person may ask you to explain the cost to interface their system to your provider's system. Perhaps the expert on your team fields that question. Before you end, ask, "Is there anything else to discuss on this topic?" If not, cross the last point off your list.

As you conclude your presentation, refer to the crossed-off list to recap the issues you addressed. By the end of your presentation, meeting your goal means having every item on the list crossed off and fully addressed.

Let's climb up to get the 10,000-foot view. This sales approach:

- fleshes out everyone's concerns;
- fully addresses each of their concerns;
- shows how your solution meets each of their concerns; and
- deals with the clients' concerns in their order of importance, not yours.

What Makes You Different?

When making a finals presentation, remember that several other competitors will be making similar presentations. Here are two ideas to make your presentation stand out from others your prospects are talking with.

1. *Differentiate yourself.* First, come prepared to offer three key things you can do for the employer and reiterate these points at the end of your meeting. Then, be sure to tie your presentation back to the original objectives you discussed with the employer's team. Address each original objective and point out how your program uniquely addresses that need.

2. *Demonstrate flexibility.* Don't be discouraged if, after all the homework you've done, you still encounter objections at the finals presentations. Be ready to counter any common objections and remember that their concerns create opportunities for you. You can address their concerns through the flexibility and strength of your program. Remember, your team members—retirement plan specialists and third-party administrators—can lend their expertise to help you develop the best solution for the client.

The bottom line: Always think in terms of helping to solve your clients' problems. Don't try to push a product.

This approach is an important aspect of the Solutions Based Selling approach that differentiates you from your competitors, so do it well.

STRATEGY 3: ASK FOR THE BUSINESS

You've selected a service provider, you're focusing on the right target market, you have all the building blocks in place, you have the right team, you've done your homework on this client, you've presented a solution that meets the client's needs, you've listened to their concerns, and you've removed any obstacles and objections.

Now it's time for the crescendo. Don't be shy or evasive: Ask for the business.

As we discussed in Chapter 5, the framework for closing the sale is an extension of Solutions Based Selling. Unfortunately, many financial professionals simply don't "close"—they don't bring the sales process to the next crucial step in the journey.

Your ultimate goal at the end of your client presentation is to ask these questions:

- Is there anything else?
- Is there anything we haven't covered in this presentation today that's not on our list and that we haven't answered?
- Does anyone have questions for any of the team members?

Address any questions or concerns that arise. "Is there anything preventing you from moving forward with us today?" or "Have I earned your business today?"

Often, the client team doesn't want to give an answer right there on the spot. Team members want to think about your presentation and, of course, compare yours with those of your competitors. If so, ask this question: "Do you need any more material?" If they say they're all set, reply this way: "Here's what I'd like to suggest; before you decide, please call one of us so we can answer any new questions or concerns. We want your business."

Reinforce this point by saying something like this: "We're not simply a retirement plan provider—we're your teammate. We're right by your side. Here's how we want this relationship to work: You do what you do best—run your business—and we'll do what we do best. If there's a change in retirement plan laws, you don't have to worry about it. We'll stay in touch with you and educate you and your employees. For example, when the new Roth 401(k) became effective, some employers worried about how to incorporate this into their plans. Please don't worry about these types of issues; we'll take care of them. You run your business and we'll run the plan."

The CEO may offer another excuse such as: "This was a great presentation. I just need to talk to my board of directors before I

Three Trial Closes to Use before Ending Your Finals Presentation

Closing is a critical step, one that's not to be skipped. You're clearly asking clients for the business. Omitting this step is probably the single biggest mistake salespeople make. You can do everything else right, but if you don't ask for the business, it may slip through your fingers.

We truly believe that the reason salespeople don't close more business is that they don't *ask* for it. At end of your finals presentations, simply ask your clients for their business. You can say something as simple as, "May we start the paperwork today?" Clients' reactions to this question can be amazing. Often, they sit back in the chair, hold a dead silence for a moment while they think, and then say yes.

Use these trial closes to take your clients' temperature at the end of finals presentations.

Trial close 1. "I've given you everything that you wanted to discuss today. We've learned that we can significantly enhance your current plan. Everyone on our team would enjoy working with your team. Would you like to move forward to the next step?"

Trial close 2. "When you originally set up your plan, it was state of the art. However, given the needs you've outlined, you've simply outgrown your plan and will be forced to make a change. From everything we've discussed, it seems clear that our plan would be a truly fantastic benefit for your organization. Do we have time to complete the paperwork today?"

Trial close 3. "Well, we've covered a lot of ground today. Given what you've shared with us, there seems to be a terrific connection between the plan we're proposing and what you're looking for. Do you agree?"

The bottom line: Often, clients are nervous about making this important buying decision. Sometimes they just need a nudge to say yes. Give them that nudge.

can accept a plan." Ask if she needs any other information. You don't want that person to go in front of the board of directors and look like she doesn't know what she's talking about. So ask if you can join that portion of the board meeting to cover the presentation. Often, you'll receive a response like this: "Our board is reluctant to bring in salespeople." Your reply: "If you need to, at any point in that meeting, call me to answer questions or explain technical concepts. We're your teammates. We want you to be confident about your presentation to your board, and we want your board to have all the pertinent information to make the best choice."

Think of the close as your watershed moment; it's the critical point at which you confidently convert your prospects into clients.

Now that you've won the business and sold an employer-sponsored retirement plan, Chapter 11 offers ways to help you retain the business using the art of follow-up. Follow-up is critical, because you'll want to grow your practice to take advantage of rollover business and ancillary sales. Following that, Chapter 12 shows you how to put all the pieces together to launch into the retirement plans business with success.

Todd's Story: A Simple Close Can Instantly Overcome Objections

After a finals presentation, I put forth this question to a business owner and his wife: "May we start the paperwork today?" The owner turned to his wife and said, "We like everything you've presented today; we just want to sleep on it."

I replied, "Great. I don't want you to feel pressured into making a decision today. I'm simply trying to figure out if this is the right solution to meet your needs. But while you're thinking about this solution, can I give you something else to consider? Think about this: Why *wouldn't* you choose us?"

They looked at each other and chuckled. She said, "I can't think of a reason not to move forward with this. Let's just do it."

The bottom line: One straightforward, action-oriented question can close the deal right then and there.

11

STICK AROUND!
THE ART OF FOLLOW-UP

"In many cases, silence is golden. Don't talk too much.
Let the client do the talking."

–Larry Sullivan, Senior Pension Consultant (retired, 36 years' experience)

Congratulations, you won the sale! Now don't go away. As a financial professional who represents employer-sponsored retirement plans, you don't get to simply sit back and count your commission checks. Selling a plan demands an ongoing relationship with the client. Some financial professionals might call this the bad news. However, as you learned in Chapter 2, every employer-sponsored retirement plan presents golden opportunities for you to sell ancillary products to the company's owner and officers. And don't forget about the hundreds of employees who, over the course of time, will leave the company and require assistance to roll over their 401(k) to an IRA. Many of these employees don't work with a financial professional and will look to you for guidance when it comes to their families' financial planning.

In this chapter, you'll learn how an ongoing education program and relationships with the company's owner and officers positions you for profitable ancillary opportunities.

ONGOING EDUCATION BUILDS TRUST

Holding initial enrollment meetings and ongoing educational meetings for plan participants is an essential step. Why? Because these meetings help employers drive up plan participation and meet their fiduciary responsibilities. Don't view these meetings as a burden. These regular interactions with business owners, officers, and plan participants help you build trust and lay the groundwork for profitable opportunities.

In Chapter 5, we discussed the employers' fiduciary responsibilities. Holding regular employee meetings on the company's retirement plan is one of the best ways to ensure that the company stays in continuous compliance with ERISA Section 404(c).

Briefly, Section 404(c) states that when an employer sponsors a retirement plan and selects funds for assets to be funded into, the employer must to do this correctly. Otherwise, the employees may sue both the individual business owner and the corporation. Therefore, the best way for a company to protect itself is to constantly reinforce employee education. When employees know about changes in the law and their retirement plan, the employer can prove that it's constantly reinforcing its responsibility as the fiduciary plan provider.

This is where you rely on your team. If the law changes, a service provider (such as The Hartford) helps you educate the employer and explain what steps to take to comply with the law. If the retirement plan changes, the provider also helps educate you, the employer, and your employees.

The art of follow-up helps you and the service provider make sure that, if changes in the law or regulations affect compliance testing issues, your client employers and their employees become informed. Example issues may be the use of safe harbor, nonelective issues, and automatic enrollment. Keep in mind that you don't need to know all the financial details about these tools. The service provider that you choose to work with will give you the tools and information to educate employers and employees, as well as to help them address any compliance testing issues.

As you've read earlier, being a good listener is highly valuable throughout the sales process. Clearly, the employer-sponsored retirement plans business isn't a cookie-cutter business; it's about solving individualized problems, even after you've closed the deal. Listening and solving problems also opens doors for profitable rollover business and ancillary sales. Keep this in mind at enrollment meetings when you're talking to individual plan participants. Ask questions, listen, and solve problems. Simultaneously, you'll gain their trust, earn their confidence, and lay a strong foundation for future business.

FOLLOW-UP GUIDELINES UNCOVER HIDDEN OPPORTUNITIES

The ongoing education program you set up for employees will cement your relationship with the plan sponsor and potentially allow you to grow your business beyond the scope of the plan. Follow-up is the least defined but arguably the most important stage of the retirement plan sales process. Once you and your team prospect, sell, design, and implement a plan, it's time to decide how you want to interact with your client on an ongoing basis. We suggest that you use the following guidelines to build trust, follow up, and uncover hidden opportunities:

- *Establish a long-term relationship.* Building a solid, long-term educational program for your client is a critical first step in building long-term trust. Be sure to set expectations up front with the employer on the content and frequency of educational sessions.
- *Engage the business owner.* Be sure to include the business owner in your educational meetings, even if it's just for five minutes at the beginning, to validate your position with the company. Plus, the business owner can help you to gather information on employees to make sure the educational sessions are as targeted and valuable as possible.

Tom's Story: How The Hartford Educated Its Team of Financial Professionals on the New Roth 401(k)

Before the Roth 401(k) became effective on January 1, 2006, we felt that a significant number of employers might be interested in incorporating this feature into their retirement plans. The Hartford prides itself on its priorities of service and education. When changes in laws or regulations affect investments, we proactively educate financial professionals in our circles, helping them implement changes in their programs and reach out to employers and employees.

To introduce and explain the Roth 401(k), we needed to create tools for three different audiences: financial professionals, plan sponsors (employers), and individual participants. We offered educational conference calls to financial professionals who represent our products. In fact, I hosted a teleseminar attended by nearly a thousand financial professionals and broker/dealer firms. In this call, I focused on "demystifying" this new retirement plan feature, and I introduced a series of practical tools to help financial professionals turn information into action and opportunity.

The Hartford team created these educational tools to spur action:

- *Roth 401(k) Study Guide for Financial Professionals.* Includes a five-step action plan to determine if the Roth 401(k) might be suitable for clients or prospects and customizable prospecting tools to support the professionals' marketing and education campaigns.
- *Roth 401(k) Employer Q&A Educational Resource Guide.* A resource tool written in layperson's terms, complete with a Roth Readiness checklist and sample employee letter to support the communication process.
- *Roth 401(k) Employer Fact Finder.* A questionnaire for financial professionals to use with employers to determine whether the Roth 401(k) feature may be a fit for their plans.
- *Participant's Guide to Understanding the Roth 401(k) Contribution Option.* A fold-out reference guide for financial professionals to give to employees with background and comparison information to determine if Roth 401(k) contributions are right for them.

Although studies and articles since the launch of the Roth 401(k) have suggested a lukewarm interest among consumers and low adoption rates by employers, The Hartford's results since the inception of the Roth

401(k) potentially indicate a different trend. In just five months, 922 Hartford employer clients implemented the Roth 401(k) into their retirement plans. We attribute this early success to a proactive, aggressive client-education campaign.

The bottom line: Select a service provider that places a priority on your education. In turn, your ongoing educational relationship with your clients helps you build trust, which directly affects retention and ancillary sales.

- *Be visible and pursue opportunities.* The participant education process is like an ongoing job interview for you when you consider other opportunities such as rollovers from retirees and job changers and referrals to family, friends, relatives, and other small business owners.
- *Schedule regular reviews.* Meet with your clients at least annually to make sure they're satisfied. Much success in client retention can be attributed to strong communication. Face-to-face contact is ideal, but teleconferences can be effective as well.
- *Set realistic client expectations.* At the inception of the plan, build a formal service agreement with the employer to clearly define your role. On a day-to-day basis, we encourage you to set realistic client expectations by "underpromising and overdelivering." Never overpromise! For example, your new client may plan to hold enrollment meetings at multiple locations throughout the nation and in Europe. Take care to set clear expectations about your attendance at these scattered locations. Don't promise to attend meetings that don't work within your schedule or budget. Instead, clarify that you'll attend the meeting at corporate headquarters in person and will attend the enrollment meetings at the various district offices by teleconference. The crux of providing great customer support is setting and managing expectations realistically. In other words, say what you do and do what you say.

- *Keep in touch.* Communicate systematically and regularly through social events or by using thank-you notes, a newsletter, and holiday cards. Be sure to always remind participants about the other financial services you provide so they'll keep you in mind for additional opportunities. Consider using this idea: Create a voice message that helps sell new products and services. For example, "Thanks for calling. I'm out of the office today and will return your call tomorrow. When we get back in touch, be sure to ask me about the following new services we've implemented . . ." Constantly reinforcing your new services will boost interest and encourage sales.
- *Solicit feedback.* Once a year, send a letter or survey to your clients and ask this question: "How are we doing? Please let us know and be honest with us." Request input on various aspects of service, products, the plan—anything your clients wish to share. This information can reap surprising insights into your products and services as well as solidify your relationships with clients. Remember, solid relationships will directly influence retention, rollover business, and ancillary sales.

Think of this aspect of "listening to your clients" as an extension of Solutions Based Selling. Use these communication touch points as opportunities to remind company officers and plan participants of the complementary services you provide.

Tom's Story: You Never Know Who the
"Millionaire Next Door" May Be

I recently spoke to a group of employers about compliance testing issues and innovative ideas. Our purpose was to ensure that these companies would uphold their fiduciary responsibilities and avoid testing problems. After the seminar, a benefits administrator asked, "Can I call you? Would you be an ongoing resource for me?"

"Of course," I agreed. He handed me his business card. This person worked for a large corporation that almost certainly had an entire staff to manage its retirement plans and this corporation fell outside of The Hartford's target market of small- to mid-size businesses. Clearly, he wasn't a prospect, but I was glad to be available to offer ideas.

A few weeks later, a benefits administrator called me. He had been an executive at this corporation and now worked at a mid-size company well within The Hartford's target market. The large-corporation benefits administrator had referred me to him. We talked about innovative ideas for the company's retirement plan. It turns out that our solutions were a perfect fit for managing his $5 million retirement plan. It was a win-win situation all around.

The bottom line: Always be professional and supportive. Provide consistent service. And never underestimate the power of word-of-mouth referrals.

12

FINAL SUGGESTIONS TO GET YOU STARTED

"Since I started with the company, retirement plans have been
an important part of our business.
We believe it can be an important part of yours."
–Tom Marra, President and CEO, Hartford Life

In previous chapters, you read about how the employer-sponsored retirement plans business is rife with opportunities to profitably grow your business. You learned how to use the Solutions Based Selling approach to prepare for a finals presentation, present solutions to meet your client's needs, and go for the close with finesse. And you learned this key idea that's worth repeating: Employer-sponsored retirement plans open doors for highly profitable rollover business and ancillary sales.

Now you may be wondering: Where do I go from here? How do I get started in this business? In this chapter, we'll show you how to build your team, mine your current list of clients, and conduct research to generate qualified leads.

STEP I: BUILD YOUR TEAM OF EXPERTS

Don't gloss over this crucial step. Invest the necessary time and research to create a winning team. Here's an action plan to build your team of experts.

Action I: Research service providers that offer employer-sponsored retirement plans. Look at trade publications and network with business leaders and other financial providers to develop a list of the big service providers that offer employer-sponsored retirement plans, such as The Hartford. Also, you can go online to glean basic information about the large companies. You can find other third-party research online as well. However, be careful. Several "objective" Web sites tout that you can enter an employer's basic information to find out which service provider offers the best plan for the lowest price. But service providers pay to participate on those Web sites.

Action 2: Create a "short list." Identify the top service providers that offer employer-sponsored retirement plans for small- to mid-size businesses and create a short list of providers to investigate further.

Action 3: Get the names of retirement plans specialists. Call each service provider on your short list and ask for the name and contact information for the retirement plans specialist who covers your territory.

Action 4: Contact the retirement plans specialist for each company on your short list. Set a time to meet with the retirement plans specialist for each of the providers you identified. If possible, meet in person, even if you need to travel to another city. Why? At end of the day, nothing or no one is more important than your retirement plans specialist.

Action 5: Ask each retirement plans specialist these questions:

- What kinds of support do you offer financial professionals who are starting to sell employer-sponsored retirement plans?
- Do you use a structured sales process?
- Do you attend client presentations with the financial professionals in your territory?
- Will you give me guidance as I prepare my presentation?
- How do you help close the sale?
- What is your company's retention rate for employer-sponsored retirement plans? (As a comparison point, The Hartford's five-year average client retention rate is 95 percent [2000 to 2005].)
- How will you help me keep my business on the books?
- What types of ancillary sales can I expect with your company?
- What processes does your company have in place to educate me, my business clients, and their employees if the law changes or the plan changes?
- Whom do you recommend as a third-party administrator?

Keep in mind that every company has a mix of phenomenal retirement plans specialists and those who are less than stellar. After each meeting, ask yourself these key questions:

- Who will help me win business?
- Who will help keep my business on the books?
- Who will help me gain ancillary business through good service?

Other points to consider are:

- With whom do I get along well?
- Who has a significant, impressive sales history and capability?
- Who do I want to put in front of my prospects?
- Who will be there when I need them?

Action 6: Select a service provider. In reality, you're selecting a retirement plans specialist who represents a service provider. The retirement plans specialist can give you ideas for selecting a third-party administrator, if necessary. (The provider may use in-

---

A Critical First Step: Research Service Providers

This book is geared toward financial professionals across the country who are ready to move from consulting and advising independent clients to working with business owners to establish employer-sponsored retirement plans. You've decided to make the move, but where do you start?

It's a good idea to start by researching what you are going to sell. Remember, you'll be partnering with the service provider you select. Do your research. Talk to the service partner's sales team. Interview retirement experts. Ask a lot of questions and make sure you're comfortable with the partner you select.

Listed here are a few resources that can help you research your options:

- *Dalbar, Inc.* Dalbar develops standards and provides research, ratings, and rankings of intangible factors to the mutual fund, broker/dealer, discount brokerage, life insurance, and banking industries. Visit the Web site at *www.dalbarinc.com.*
- *A.M. Best.* A Best's Financial Strength Rating is an independent opinion, based on a comprehensive quantitative and qualitative evaluation of a company's balance sheet, operating performance, and business profile. Find the information at *www.ambest.com/ratings/guide.html.*
- *Standard & Poor's.* A credit ratings search on Standard & Poor's Web site will provide the current Standard & Poor's ratings for issuers, instruments, and bond funds. You'll also be able to look up corporate governance scores and service evaluations. This Web site is *www.standardandpoors.com.*
- *Moody's.* Moody's Web site offers registered users ratings on corporate, government, and structured finance securities; current ratings news; and watch lists. The Web site is *www.moodys.com.*

The bottom line: Researching service providers before selecting one is a critical step to success in this business.

house administrators.) Remember, this business isn't about products, it's about people. Find the best people for your team.

STEP 2: MINE YOUR LIST OF CURRENT CLIENTS

In your practice right now, you conduct annual reviews with your clients and their spouses. You probably offer guidance and help them manage their 401(k) plans through their selection of asset allocations. You provide this service free of charge.

Isn't it time to start getting paid for this?

If your clients need education to select their asset allocation, think of this is a big waving flag—their companies aren't educating them about their retirement plans. Certainly you can do a better job and provide a better product. Recall the story of the manufacturing company's employee who became so excited about a potential new plan, the benefits administrator was forced to review the company's retirement plan. Lo and behold, the plan was out of date and wasn't being serviced. Look at your annual reviews with current clients as an excellent jumping-off point to get new clients and grow your business with employer-sponsored retirement plans.

Ask these questions: Who is your company contact for your 401(k) plan? Who runs the retirement plan on a day-to-day basis? May I give that person your name as a referral? Then contact the plan administrator and go after that business.

Of course, when mining your list of current clients, be sure to identify doctors, attorneys, dentists, and other business owners. Some financial professionals refuse to work with companies that have retirement plans valued at less than $100,000. Don't be afraid to go for "singles" and "doubles"—these can turn into "home runs" later.

We recommend that you start with small companies and provide great service for those accounts. Many of these client accounts can grow to become $5 or $10 million accounts, generating long-term profits and reaping lucrative ancillary business.

You May Be Doing Business with Your Best Prospects

Certainly Steve, a financial professional with a broker/dealer firm in De-Forest, Wisconsin, was already doing business with his best prospects. In fact, a routine visit to the dentist turned into a 401(k) sale and referrals to other area dentists.

Steve and his dentist have been mutual clients for years. A few years ago, Steve created a group disability plan for the dental practice and provided personal financial planning for some of the employees. The dentist's profit-sharing plan was transferred to a new provider when his existing provider got out of the business. The dentist and his employees grew increasingly dissatisfied with the new provider's level of service. That's when the dentist called Steve.

In Steve's presentation, he suggested the dentist change from a profit-sharing plan to a 401(k) so employees could make additional deferrals into their accounts. He also suggested that the plan be changed to a cross-tested formula, so the dentist could continue to contribute the same dollar amount to the plan while receiving more of the plan contributions.

The dentist was impressed with this solution, and Steve's relationship with him was cemented. Since the plan closed, Steve has been available to help the dental employees with rollovers and life insurance. Steve is also helping the dentist with a buyout arrangement using life insurance. And he has asked for a positive referral to other dentists in the area.

The bottom line: Don't overlook the potential for finding prospects among the people with whom you routinely do business.

STEP 3: USE DATA-MINING SERVICES TO GENERATE QUALIFIED LISTS

As you read in Chapter 4, you can run reports from data-mining services such as Larkspur DataMaster Pro, Judy Diamond, and FreeERISA.com to generate qualified lists in your target market. These services sweep the data from companies' IRS Forms 5500 and provide key details for companies that currently run retirement plans. Using these services, the sky's the limit for opportunities. And it's easy to get started. Once you're comfortable using this research approach, you can find potential sales opportunities throughout your region.

THE SKY'S THE LIMIT . . .

Now you're ready to start. We encourage you to dive in. Don't wait for a "better time"—there has never been a better time in history to enter this lucrative market. Employer-sponsored retirement plans offer a "sky's the limit" opportunity to grow your business profitably.

WALK A MILE IN FRANK'S SHOES

13

FICTIONAL CASE STUDY THAT REVEALS STEPS TO PROSPECT, OVERCOME OBJECTIONS, AND WIN SALES

You're intrigued about the employee-sponsored retirement plans market. And you appreciate the earnings potential and opportunities to grow your business. But you still have a few burning questions before you're ready to dive in. For example:

- Exactly how do I get started? How do I prospect for clients and get them to agree to an initial sit-down discussion, let alone get someone to agree happily to a full-length presentation?
- How do I overcome clients' objections?
- How do I smoothly deliver a close, get a client to say yes, and win the sale?

Meet Frank, a financial professional who works for a broker/ dealer firm in Colorado Springs, Colorado. Learn from Frank's successes (and mistakes) as he moves through the steps to sell employer-sponsored retirement plans.

Throughout, Frank is mentored by Rick, a retirement plans specialist (also referred to as a regional sales director) for a major service provider. Rick is headquartered in Denver, Colorado, and supports financial professionals throughout his territory. While recruiting financial professionals to sell employer-sponsored retirement plans, Rick held an initial discussion with Frank by telephone. Frank was receptive. After switching careers, Frank has been a financial professional for three years. Always interested in learning more about the business—and discovering additional earning opportunities—Frank agreed to meet with Rick.

Join Frank on his journey as he enters the employer-sponsored retirement plans market, learns how to overcome clients' objections, and discovers how to use Solutions Based Selling to close deals and win sales.

STEP 1: RICK CONVINCES FRANK HE NEEDS TO SELL RETIREMENT PLANS

Rick Offers Information and Assistance

It's a beautiful, crisp Colorado morning as Rick travels south on I-25 from Denver, making his way to his first appointment in Colorado Springs. Rick and Frank agreed to meet and have breakfast at a local restaurant before the stock market opened. They meet in person for the first time at Mike's Mountain Café, a favorite eatery in the foothills of Pikes Peak.

"Frank, I really appreciate you meeting me here," Rick says. "This gives us an opportunity to discuss a few things."

"No problem," Frank says. "I'm always looking for a good idea."

"Frank, how long have you been in this business?" Rick asks.

"Three years. I've been pretty successful so far. I guess one reason is that I'm always open to new ideas—new ways to build my business."

After they order breakfast, Rick asks Frank about his business and clients. He also asks about Frank's family and how he likes to enjoy his free time. Rick wants to get to know Frank as a person as well as a businessperson. He listens as Frank recounts stories about his three children, now in their teens and approaching their college years, and the family's annual trips to explore the "four corners" of the world.

When their breakfast arrives, Frank asks, "So, Rick, what ideas can you share with me today?"

"I'd like to ask you a couple more questions before I give you my ideas," Rick replies.

"Sure, go ahead."

"Frank, how many employer-sponsored retirement plans do you have in your book of business?"

"I just have one."

"How are things going with that plan?" Rick asks.

"It's going great but, to be truthful, I've decided not to sell any more retirement plans in my business," Frank says.

"Why not?"

"Because retirement plans take too long to sell." In his experience, sales took nearly a year to close. Other financial professionals have also told him that their sales cycles have taken years!

"Well, sometimes these plans do have long sales cycles," Rick responds. "But it doesn't have to be *that* long. With increases in technology and investor sophistication, we find that the sales cycle on employer-sponsored retirement plans is usually only three to four months."

"Really?" says Frank. "I never would have guessed that."

"Approached the wrong way, these plans can take a year or two to sell," Rick explains. "However, if you take the right approach, you can shorten the sales cycle significantly in most cases."

Frank pondered that for a moment. "That's great, but I'll be honest with you, Rick. The retirement plans market seems too complex. There's a maze of federal and state laws to follow. I'm not really comfortable with all that. It seems too risky. A couple of times I tried to sell retirement plans, and the employers asked extremely technical questions. I didn't know the answers—I felt foolish."

"Frank, I completely understand where you're coming from. I meet with financial professionals like you every week and hear these common concerns a lot. That's why it's important to work with a 'retirement plans geek' like me. By combining my knowledge and skills in the retirement plans arena with your contacts and marketing skills, we can earn a lot more business together."

"You're telling me that you'll actually meet with my clients and help me sell retirement plans?" Frank asks.

"That's exactly what I'm saying. If you find a prospect who's willing to sit down and talk with us, I'm willing to drive down from Denver to meet with your clients and prospects and help you win the business."

"Wow, that's great." Pausing a moment, Frank adds, "I'm sure you must have a minimum requirement for the plan size before you'll drive down here. Is that right?"

"All we have to do is ensure your prospect meets the underwriting criteria our company has established. If so, I'll drive to the Springs and help you close the business—whether it's a start-up plan for a family-owned business or a large plan for a high-tech company."

"Hmm, I might be willing to give this a shot," Frank says. "Although I have another concern. The veterans in my office have mentioned that the closing rate on retirement plans is terrible. That's another reason I've stayed away from selling them."

Rick lays it on the line. "Frank, there are many different ways to build your business and many different products you can offer. Retirement plan sales isn't for everyone. But because so many people in our industry have the misconception that the closing rate is too low and the sales cycle is too long, this actually creates an environment that makes it easy to sell retirement plans—you're competing with fewer people. Also, most financial professionals are used to doing everything themselves. In their efforts to sell employer-sponsored retirement plans, they simply don't rely on the services of a retirement plans specialist like me. I've found that winning business goes up fourfold when I'm in the meetings. Please don't take that the wrong way, Frank. We'd be working as a team—combining my knowledge and skills with your contacts and marketing abilities. That's how we win business."

Frank pauses for a moment, absorbing the idea of adding retirement plans to his current menu of product and service offerings. "Well, Rick, this has been enlightening. You've opened my eyes a bit. I've wondered how much opportunity there really is with the retirement plans business. Plus, I've discovered something with the one plan I *did* sell—once I tapped into that company through its retirement plan, I gained access to all the employees. Since then, several well-paid executives have come to me for financial guidance and have become clients. I'd like to give this a try. But I have to admit, I have no idea how get started."

As Rick calculates the tip and pays the restaurant bill, he asks, "Frank, how many business owners do you have in your book of business?"

"Well, I've been in this business for three years. I probably only have six or eight business owners in my book," he admits.

"Okay, let's focus on that list first. Let's go back to your office and continue our conversation."

Research Sparks Brainstorming about Solutions

At Frank's office, Rick takes a legal pad out of his briefcase and asks Frank to write down the names of his clients who own businesses and those companies' names.

"What are you going to do with this list?" Frank asks.

"I'm going to show you how to research information about these companies' retirement plans." Rick says. "We'll make notes here, then I'll give you this pad to continue your information search. So first, go to *www.FreeERISA.com* on your computer. This is a database you can use to research corporate retirement plans. Now let's look at another research tool called the Larkspur DataMaster Pro. My company will give you access via our subscription."

"Wow, look at all this information!" Frank says. "Where do these databases get their information?"

"The information comes from corporate tax returns that companies must file on their retirement plans."

"That's public information?"

"Yes, absolutely. Let's pull up the first company name on your list."

Frank types the company name and hits "search." The search results show a long list of companies across the country with this same business name. Rick shows Frank how to refine the search by adding "Colorado Springs" in the city field and "Colorado" in the state field. This time, the search results reveal just one company. Frank clicks to see the full information about this company's retirement plan.

"Wow," says Frank. "Look at all this information: my client's name, the amount of assets in his retirement plan, the current provider . . ."

Rick adds, "Yes, this is a great tool. But the first thing to look at is the date of the report. Notice that this information is two years old. Thus, some of this information may no longer be accurate. Keep in mind when you're looking at these reports that the company may not be with the same provider. Consider that total assets will have changed and that the decision maker could have left the company. Clearly, all this information is subject to change. This database gives us a picture of what the company's plan looked like at that date."

"Why is this information so old if it comes from tax returns?" Frank wonders aloud.

"Some companies don't file their tax returns until October of the following year. After that, it takes time for these data companies to acquire the information and update their databases. Remember, this database provides guidance to financial professionals—so don't interpret this as today's scenario . . . Frank, notice here that your client's company has a money purchase plan."

"What does that mean?"

"If the company still has a money purchase plan, here's how you can help your client. Money purchase plans were popular for many years because they allowed business owners to contribute up to twenty-five percent of their salary for their retirement years. But there are a couple of downsides. The company must commit to a fixed contribution and make that payment to the plan every year, even if the company doesn't earn a profit in a given year. Another disadvantage is that employees can only make contributions to this plan on an after-tax basis."

"Why don't they just have a 401(k) profit-sharing plan?" Frank asks. "Wouldn't that allow the employer to make discretionary annual contributions and allow employees to make pretax contributions that will grow tax-free?"

"Yes, that's right," Rick responds. "But when your client put this plan in place, the maximum amount that could be contributed to a 401(k) profit-sharing plan was fifteen percent. That's probably why your client elected to go with a money purchase plan. Businesses can now contribute up to twenty-five percent and that calculation no longer includes employee deferrals."

"What would we recommend to my client . . . freeze the money purchase plan and start a new 401(k)?"

"No," Rick responds. "We can simply convert the money purchase plan into a 401(k) profit-sharing plan. This plan design would give your client all the advantages of his current money purchase plan—and create new opportunities for employees to defer on a pretax basis or on a Roth basis. Plus, this plan would remove the requirement to contribute a fixed amount every year, which would give your client the flexibility to increase or decrease the company's contribution, depending on the company's performance that year."

"Wow, that sounds great. That would be a great solution for him, especially during tough economic times. But I'm not sure I'll remember all these details."

"You don't have to, Frank. Remember, you'll manage the relationship. Get me in front of your client. I'll go through this same scenario with him—and I hope he'll get as excited about it as you are."

Frank turns his attention to the database report and notices his client's company retirement plan serviced 40 employees and had over $1 million in assets at the report date.

"Do you know how many individual plans I have to open to gather a million dollars in assets?" Frank asks.

"That's one of the beauties of selling retirement plans," says Rick. "One sale typically lands you a large amount of assets. Plus, it's like adding 40 new clients. These employees probably have outside monies that you can help them invest."

"I never knew I could get this excited about corporate retirement plans," Frank smiles. "Let's look up my next client . . ."

Three Ideas to Get Started

Frank and Rick research all the companies on Frank's list and then discuss other ways to prospect retirement plans. Rick gives Frank three ideas.

Idea 1: "It's time to start getting paid for consulting on your clients' 401(k) plans." Many of Frank's current clients ask for his help to manage their assets in their companies' 401(k) plans, which Frank does willingly. Rick hands Frank a stack of sample statements that are informative and easy to read. When Frank helps clients with their retirement accounts, he should pull out the sample statement and ask them to take a minute to page through it. Then Frank should ask, "Wouldn't you rather get statements that look like this?"

When a client says yes, Frank can ask for the name of the person who manages the company's retirement plan on a day-to-day basis and ask the client for permission to use her name as a reference. He'll call the retirement plan administrator and explain that his client (a coworker) has asked him to help select assets for the retirement plan. He'll ask to meet with the administrator to provide better guidance on the client's accounts.

When Frank meets with the administrator, he'll ask questions such as, "What do you like best about the current retirement plan provider?" "What would you like to see improved?" and "Have your employees lodged any complaints about this plan?" Then

Frank will ask if the administrator would be willing to looking at an alternative to the current plan.

Idea 2: "When business owners ask you for investment tips, turn the conversation into an opportunity to discuss their retirement plans." Rick learns that Frank is a member of several fraternal organizations and the Colorado Springs Chamber of Commerce. They share stories about how business owners with whom they network often ask, "How's the market doing today?" or "Got any hot investment tips?"

Frank chuckles. "I hear that all the time! I've learned that this is just a conversation starter; they're not really looking for investment tips."

"That's been my experience, too," says Rick. "The next time a business owner or decision maker asks you for an investment tip, turn the tables and say, 'Now let me ask you a question: What areas of your retirement plan would you like to see improved?' After you have this discussion, say, 'I know this isn't the appropriate time or place, but if I were to call you or your assistant, would you schedule 15 to 20 minutes to continue this conversation? Would you grant me that time? I may have an idea that would interest you.'"

Idea 3: "Use Larkspur DataMaster Pro to create a short, focused, and fruitful list of prospects." Rick shows Frank how to enter specific search criteria in the database such as city name, zip code, area code, level of assets, number of participants, and a host of other factors. "Focus on specific search criteria," Rick advises. "If your prospecting list gets too big, it becomes confusing and overwhelming."

Frank Agrees to Make Some Calls

Rick and Frank agree to focus Frank's prospecting efforts on his list of eight clients who own businesses. Frank agrees to contact these clients in the next two days. They schedule a phone meeting to follow up on Frank's prospecting.

"I have one more question," Frank says. "What do I say to my clients when I call? Do I just ask if I can get a shot at their retirement plans?"

"Frank, you can approach this different ways. One way is simply to ask them what they like and dislike about their current retirement plan, then ask if they would give you an opportunity to present a few new ideas. Another is to take a step back and ask, 'If you had to rate my services on a scale of one to ten, how well would you say I'm servicing your account?' Assuming they don't say two," Rick says, laughing, "if they answer eight or ten, ask them if they would give you the opportunity to provide their employees that same level of service by showing how you can help with the company's retirement plan."

"That's it? That's all I need to do?" Frank says.

"That's all you need to do," Rick confirms. "Just try to get the initial appointment and meet with them."

"Then what?"

"Ah, grasshopper . . . one step at a time," Rick teases. "Set up the initial appointments with these clients. When we talk in two days, we'll discuss our next steps."

STEP 2: FRANK GOES PROSPECTING

Unpleasant Surprises

"I scheduled two appointments, and I think I'll get two more," Frank reports when Rick calls two days later. Frank adds that one of his clients has been with his current retirement plan provider for several years. "I was shocked to find out that I didn't have all of his business; another broker has been getting most of my client's investment money. I'm concerned I may lose the account."

"That's not uncommon," Rick says. "A lot of financial providers who sell retirement plans often get the business owners' personal accounts and take away the business from the original financial provider."

"Here's the worst part. I found out that three of my other clients all moved their retirement plans in the last year or so. They didn't know I could sell retirement plans. I've never felt so foolish in my life, knowing that those three plans could've been mine."

"I'm sorry to hear that," Rick says. "Unless the plans are terrible, those clients probably won't be ready to make a change this soon. But don't worry; all hope isn't lost. Call them back, find out if they're satisfied with the level of attention they're getting, or if they'd like to see more communication and education for their employees. Maybe you can get them to change the broker of record over to you."

"Thanks, Rick, that's a great idea."

"So we have two appointments to get started," Rick says. "Let's talk about our next steps."

Information-Gathering Form and Diagnostic Worksheet

Frank explains that one of the appointments is with the manufacturing company with the money purchase plan that they researched together. The other appointment is with a dental practice. It currently has a 401(k) profit-sharing plan for the dentist and her employees. Rick e-mailed an information-gathering form and a diagnostic worksheet to Frank for him to use with these clients.

"I want to make sure you're comfortable asking these questions and completing these forms when you meet with them," Rick says.

Frank opens the files and looks at the information-gathering form, then tells Rick, "These are basic questions about the provider and whether they're happy with the service. Yes, I'm comfortable asking these questions."

"The diagnostic worksheet is even more important than the information-gathering form," Rick replies. "We use this form to gauge our potential success rate before we even go in and make a presentation. It tells us whether we've done enough homework to take our one shot at getting the business. Frank, one of the most common mistakes financial professionals make is going after the business too early—before they've done all their homework. So we'll have our work cut out for us. When are your appointments?"

"My first appointment is later today and my second one is scheduled for tomorrow morning." They decide to talk again after Frank has met with both business owners.

STEP 3: FRANK MEETS WITH TWO PROSPECTIVE CLIENTS

The Manufacturing Firm

That afternoon, Frank meets with Bob, the owner of a manufacturing company with 40 employees. Frank first confirms that Bob still has the money purchase plan that the database revealed. Then he asks, "Bob, which features of this plan do you like best, and which are the most important for you?"

"I can't say anything really good or bad about this profit-sharing plan. I just know it's a great way to get personal tax deductions while diversifying my net worth."

"Tell me more about the personal tax savings," Frank asks. "Are you saving as much in the retirement plan as you would like?"

"To tell you the truth, I wouldn't mind increasing the amount."

"Bob, if you could pick any number, how much in pretax dollars would you like to put in this plan for yourself?"

"Well, if I could, I'd like to save at least thirty thousand dollars a year," Bob says. "The law says I'm supposed to put the same percentage in for me and for each of my employees. With 40 employees, that would be an insane amount. Plus, with our current plan, I have to put the same percentage in every year; I don't have the flexibility to change that."

"Is that a concern for you?" Frank asks.

"Yeah, because we've had a few lean years. I had to borrow money just to make those contributions, and it was difficult to pay on the loans. But we've had phenomenal years, too. I'd like to be able to put more toward my personal retirement in the good years."

"Great. Tell me, Bob, in your current retirement program, what areas would you like to improve?" Frank asks.

"In addition to what I already told you, I currently manage all the money for the employees, and I'm uncomfortable with that," Bob admits. "I'd rather they make their own investment decisions so I don't have that liability."

"Well, Bob, if I could show you an alternative program that allows you to save more money, have the flexibility to contribute less in lean years, and allows your employees to make their own decisions about their accounts, is there any reason why you wouldn't change plans?"

"Well, yes. I simply can't afford to have both plans!"

Smiling, Frank explains, "That's the beauty of this, Bob, we're not talking about adding a second plan. We're talking about converting your current plan to a new plan that allows you to save more money, has more flexibility, and delegates investment decisions to your employees. So based on that criteria, is there any *other* reason you wouldn't change your plan?"

"Well, we just changed plans twelve years ago. It's probably too soon."

"While it's only been twelve years, if I could prove to you beyond any doubt in your mind that there are significant reasons for you to change your plan today, is there any other reason that would prohibit you from changing plans?"

"I guess I feel stuck," Bob says. "My attorney says I can't change plans, according to some IRS subsection code."

"Well, I'm not sure what your attorney might be thinking. I have a gentleman on my team named Rick; he's my retirement plans expert, and he can explain how all this works. I call him my 'retirement plans geek.' If we can convince your attorney to make the change, would you change plans?"

"If you can do all that, I'd definitely be willing to change plans," Bob answers.

"Who handles the current retirement plan on a day-to-day basis? And can I speak to that person to gather more information?"

"That's Suzanne, my CFO," Bob replies.

"I don't know if this would be the appropriate time, but I'd love to talk with her soon. Would you call Suzanne and see if she has ten or fifteen minutes to sit down with me today or another day?"

As Bob is calling Suzanne, Frank thinks, "So far, this is way too easy."

Bob hangs up the phone and relays Suzanne's message: "When the boss calls, she makes the time." Bob escorts Frank down the hall to Suzanne's office, introduces the two of them, and explains that Frank needs a few minutes of her time to gather information on the company's retirement plan. Then he excuses himself to pay attention to the day's issues.

"It's nice to meet you," Suzanne says. "But I need to tell you, I really have very little time. I have a lot of respect for Bob. Whenever the boss calls, I find a way to carve out time for his requests. But let's keep this meeting as short as possible. What would you like to know about our retirement plan?"

Frank pulls out a clean information-gathering form and asks, "What do you like best about your current retirement plan?"

Suzanne scoffs, "Nothing!"

"You're obviously not happy with the plan; what areas would you like to see improved?"

"The service. I can never get a phone call or e-mail returned. Once we made the decision to go with that company, they felt they didn't need to service our plan," she says, clearly showing her frustration.

During the next 15 minutes, Frank learns everything he can about the company's money purchase plan, including the names of those involved: the financial professional, third-party administrator, and service provider. He discovers that the employees complain because they only get one statement a year and they have no say in how their money is invested. In addition, Suzanne has to pass out the statements herself, an extra responsibility she doesn't like.

"Forty statements may not seem like a lot," she explains. "But this is private information, so I have to hand out each statement in person. If employees are out sick or on vacation, I have to try to catch them later. I simply don't have time for that."

After Frank gathers the information, he thanks Suzanne for her time and heads back to his car. He immediately calls Rick to give him a progress report.

"I thought you had two meetings scheduled and that we'd talk after the second meeting?" Rick asks.

"Yes, that's right. But I just wanted to tell you—this isn't nearly as hard as I thought it would be. If the second meeting goes this well, I think we'll make these sales happen."

The Dentist's Office

The next morning, Frank prepares for his meeting with Laura, the dentist who owns a dental practice in Colorado Springs.

Arriving at her office at the appointed hour, Frank thanks Laura for taking the time to meet with him.

"Frank, you know I'll always make time for you," Laura responds warmly. "You said you had some questions for me, but didn't go into details. I rated you a perfect ten for service, and you mentioned you're going to somehow give my employees that same level of service. I'm curious—how do you plan to make that happen?" She smiles as she challenges him.

Frank confirms with Laura that her dental practice has a $4 million 401(k) profit-sharing plan. Frank then asks the first of four "magic" questions.

"What do you like best about your current retirement plan?" Laura explains that she recently made changes to her program and now has a cross-tested plan, which allows the business to contribute more money for her than for the nonowners of the company.

"Why is that important to you?" Frank asks.

"I'm trying to save as much as I can for my retirement," Laura replies. "But I certainly don't want to save that same amount of money for each of my employees—that wouldn't be feasible."

"What else do you like about your current plan?"

"It seems to be easy to use, I get regular statements, I can retrieve information on the company's Internet site, and my employees can manage their own money," she notes.

"Laura, if you could wave a magic wand over your retirement plan, what improvements would you make?"

"First of all, I'd want to ensure my fiduciary responsibilities are covered. While I don't exactly understand what these are, I'm concerned that I have some exposure. At my last annual dental conference, the big buzz among dentists is the liability we may have if we don't properly fulfill our fiduciary responsibilities. So my first 'magic wand' request would be to know that I don't have to worry about any liabilities associated with my retirement plan. More important, though, my second 'magic wand' request would be to save a lot more money than I am today. I'm over fifty now, and my plan only allows me to save thirty thousand dollars a year—that's just not enough to reach my retirement goals."

"If there were no limit, how much would you like to save each year?" Frank asks.

"No limit? As much as I can!"

Frank laughs. "Realistically, Laura, how much?"

Laura thinks for a moment and says that she'd like to save $150,000 or $200,000 a year.

"What else would you like to see improved in your plan?" Frank asks.

"Well, I'm concerned that my employees aren't getting enough assistance and education to make good decisions about how to invest their money."

"Let me ask you a question, Laura. Would you let your employees manage the funds in your account? Would you feel comfortable letting them select the asset allocations?"

"No way."

"If you don't think they're qualified to manage your account, how are they qualified to manage their own?" Frank asks.

"That's my feeling exactly," she responds.

"Do you have any concerns about converting your plan?" Franks asks.

"Yes. While I'm not thrilled with my current situation and you *have* generated interest from me, I'm worried about moving from a bad situation to a worse situation."

"Let me guess. You skipped that class in dental school that covered your dental practices retirement plan decisions, right?"

"While I don't trust my ability to make the right decision, I have a feeling that I need to delegate this process, Frank."

"If I showed you an alternative to your 401(k) profit-sharing plan that still allows you to cross-test your plan, potentially allows you to save one hundred and fifty thousand dollars a year, and helps you meet your fiduciary responsibilities, would you change plans?"

Laura laughs, "If you show me how to save that much every year, I'll hand the plan to you on a silver platter."

"Great. I need to gather a little more information about your retirement plan. Who handles the plan on a day-to-day basis?"

"We don't have a benefits administrator. I handle it all myself. What would you like to know?"

Within 20 minutes, Laura provides all the information Frank needs to answer the questions on his information-gathering form. However, one thought needles him: Did he just promise something he can't deliver?

Frank and Rick Debrief

"I may have suggested we could offer something we can't," Frank admits to Rick during their afternoon call.

"What was that?"

"Well, my second appointment was with my client, Laura, the dentist," Frank says. "She wants to save more money than she's saving right now."

"That's not unusual. How much would she like to save?"

"She'd like to save a hundred and fifty thousand a year—or more."

"How much did you tell her she *could* save?" Rick asks.

"I didn't give her a specific amount; I just asked her to name a target."

Rick assures Frank that all is not lost. They sift through the notes on the information-gathering forms, then work through the diagnostic worksheet for each prospect. They agree to move forward with both clients. Frank agrees to set appointments for the following week.

"Before we meet with your clients, I'd like you to prepare to talk about how you can help employees who participate in our retirement plans and how you're willing to service this plan," Rick says.

"What do you mean?"

"Are you willing to meet one on one with each employee?" Rick says. "Are you willing to take the time to do that? How often would you visit each company to meet with the participants as a group? Will you commit to providing ongoing educational seminars? I want you to put your service commitment into a written document. During our meetings, you'll be ready to hand this service document to your clients."

"Okay," Frank agrees. "What else?"

"That's it for now. That's your role. Your number-one job is to maintain the relationship with the business owners and their employees."

"That's it?" Frank asks incredulously.

"There are more details, but I want you to keep in mind that your first and foremost job is to service your accounts. Keep the people happy and manage the relationships. By far, this is the most important thing you can do. Your second responsibility is to make sure the employees have all the information and education they need to make good decisions about managing their money."

"That seems too easy; that's what I do every day," Frank says.

"Exactly!"

STEP 4: FRANK AND RICK PRESENT SOLUTIONS IN TWO FINALS PRESENTATIONS

The Manufacturing Firm

It's a blustery day in the Pikes Peak foothills when Rick and Frank meet Bob and Suzanne at the manufacturing company. After they get settled in the conference room with hot coffee, Frank thanks Bob and Suzanne for providing the opportunity to show them an alternative to their current retirement plan.

"Before we get started, let me introduce Rick, my retirement plans specialist," Frank says. "He's the retirement plans geek I mentioned last week." Everyone laughs. Frank then introduces Bob and Suzanne to Rick, noting their roles with the company's retirement plan.

Next, Frank confirms that Bob and Suzanne still have 1½ hours to meet, as they agreed when he set the appointment. He then asks permission to use the dry-eraser board.

Frank turns to the business owner and says, "Bob, what are your specific goals for this meeting?"

"You had mentioned being able to solve my problem regarding flexibility in a profit-sharing plan in both good years and lean years," Bob says. "I'm curious to find out how you can do that."

"Anything else, Bob?"

"I'm sure I'll have other questions, but that's my main concern."

Frank turns to Suzanne and asks, "Suzanne, what would you like to accomplish in this meeting?"

"Well, I need to see how your fees and expenses compare to our current plan. And we need to review your mutual fund lineup."

Surprised, Frank says, "Great, we'll make sure we cover that. First, though, I'd like to recap what we talked about in our first meeting. Suzanne, you expressed that you were extremely frustrated with your current plan. You're experiencing severe service issues, and employees are complaining that they only receive one statement a year and aren't allowed to manage their own money. Why do you say you're curious about our mutual fund lineup and our plan's fees and expenses?"

"Well, Frank, I consider myself a fairly smart cookie, but I don't know much about employer-sponsored retirement plans," Suzanne admits. "I'm nervous . . . the thought of switching makes my stomach turn. What if we make the move—go with your new plan—but we get stuck with an expensive plan and funds that don't perform? What if it turns out that we should've just stayed with our current provider and put up with the bad service?"

"I understand your concerns, Suzanne. Most people in your shoes feel the same way you do. But why, exactly, do you feel you need to focus on fees and performance?"

"Isn't that what you're supposed to look at when a vendor presents an alternative plan?"

Rick chimes in and says, "Suzanne, you've actually struck an important chord here. The majority of people consider making a change with their retirement plans because they're disgusted with service. Yet when we present to them, instead of focusing on service and asking, 'How will you fix my service problems?' they immediately turn to questions about fees and expenses. It's what people have been programmed to ask. Let's face it, Suzanne, you probably have four to six years of college and a lot of on-the-job experience. But you've probably never received specific training in your career on how to select a retirement plan."

Suzanne chuckles, "No, I haven't."

"The foremost money magazines and newspapers report that this business is all about fees and expenses," Rick adds. "I won't suggest those aren't important considerations, because they are. However, in my opinion, instead of being the leading decision factors for most employers, they should play a supporting role. Your primary reason for making the decision should be to address the issue at hand: that is, who can do the best job of resolving your service issues and taking you to a better place."

"So, Rick, are you saying that because I'm really unhappy with the service, I should make sure you tell me exactly how you'll address my problems: getting phone calls returned, receiving statements more frequently, and sending statements to employees' homes?"

Rick smiles and says, "Exactly. We still need to discuss fees, performance, and anything else you deem important. And we'll have those discussions along with our conversation on service. Suzanne, what if I brought you the lowest-priced plan on the street or provided funds with the best performance, but I never returned your phone calls? Would you be happy?"

"No, absolutely not. I see your point, Rick."

"Just to be clear, let's list all of your goals on the eraser board," Rick says. "Goal number one: Bob, you want more flexibility for the company to contribute in good years and lean years. In other words, you want to find out how to convert the current money purchase plan to a 401(k) plan that offers discretionary contributions. Is that right?"

"Yes."

"Goal number two: Suzanne, you want to feel confident you'll get better service with the new plan. You want to find out how often our statements come out, how easy they are for employees to understand, and whether they'll be sent directly to employees' homes or you'll have to pass them out. Plus, you want to address how much this solution will cost and discuss fund performance. And you mentioned that employees would like to take control of their own accounts. Is that right, Suzanne?"

"Yes."

Point by point, Rick addresses each goal. He proposes that they convert the company's money purchase plan to a 401(k) profit-sharing plan. He explains how the conversion would occur and how they would support the initial enrollment process. Frank gives Bob and Suzanne a copy of his service commitment and explains how his team will provide ongoing support, tools, resources, and education. The service commitment is designed to make sure that plan participants understand how much they need to save to achieve their retirement goals and how to diversify their individual accounts properly.

After discussing each goal, Rick stops the presentation to make sure he completely addresses Bob and Suzanne's questions and concerns. He asks Bob and Suzanne: "Would you be completely satisfied if we give you the feature I just described to address this particular issue?" Point by point, Bob and Suzanne agree that the plan Rick is presenting would be a great solution for their problems.

Near the end of his presentation, Rick touches on other items they hadn't mentioned but that he has incorporated into his proposal. After reviewing the plan's fees and expenses, Rick turns to Suzanne and asks, "Based on the quality program we've talked about today, do you feel that our fee proposal is fair?"

"Yes, I do," Suzanne says.

Rick addresses both clients and asks, "Bob and Suzanne, do you have any concerns? Is there anything that would prevent you from moving your plan over to Frank and me?"

Bob and Suzanne look at each other.

"Suzanne, what are your thoughts?" Bob asks.

"Bob, this is your company; this is your decision. But this plan seems to make sense for our company. Plus, it'll save me a lot of grief. I have no reservations about moving forward."

Bob turns to Frank and says, "Frank, you know, I was curious to hear your proposal, but I wasn't prepared to make a decision today. We have some front-burner issues in the plant that I need to address before anything else. However, I didn't know Suzanne was going through this service nightmare. She was sheltering me from several serious issues and employee complaints. I learned something new today."

"Bob, that's why you delegate things to me. I handle them. I don't want to be in your office complaining," Suzanne replies.

"I've noticed Suzanne is lighting up like a Christmas tree about this plan," Bob continues. "I can tell she's excited about making this change. I don't see any reason why we shouldn't move forward."

"Bob and Suzanne, is today the appropriate day to complete the paperwork, or should we schedule a different day this week?" Rick says.

"Well, how long will it take?" Bob asks.

"There are some plan design issues we need to address," Rick replies. "This would extend our meeting by another hour."

"Bob, I'd like to do this now, while everything is fresh in my mind," Suzanne says. "I can make the time if you can."

"Let me think for a moment." Bob leans back in his chair. "I have some problems in the shop I need to address before the end of the day. But I agree with Suzanne; let's keep going while this is fresh in our minds."

An hour later, Rick and Frank do a high-five as they walk across the parking lot.

"We're one for one," Rick says, "but we can't count on that instant success all the time."

"Yeah," Frank agrees, feeling optimistic. "But that doesn't mean we can't be two for two." And he gives Rick another high-five.

Interlude

As they drive to their second appointment, Rick asks Frank, "Was there anything I did that made you uncomfortable in our meeting with Bob and Suzanne? I want to make sure you're happy with how I conducted the meeting. I can smooth out any wrinkles for our presentation to Laura."

"No, in fact, I have to compliment you. When they threw out an objection, you didn't get defensive. By thoroughly discussing each point with them, they essentially answered their own objections. But what I really liked is that you were always closing. After every point, you asked each of them if they had any concerns or reservations. It was highly effective. I'm going to use those same techniques in sales situations with my other clients. Plus, I'm really glad you were there. Some of Suzanne's questions were fairly technical. It felt to me like she was talking a foreign language. But you knew in general what she was asking and gave clear responses to all of her questions."

Rick laughs and says, "I guess I lived up to my title of being a retirement plans geek."

The Dentist's Office

Laura is finishing with a client when Frank and Rick arrive, so Rick uses the opportunity to chat with the receptionist, Marie, and get her point of view on the dental practice's retirement plan.

"Are you going to fix our retirement plan?" Marie asks.

"Well, what do you think needs fixing?" Rick asks.

"Nobody helps us. I never know how to invest my money. I don't have any investments outside of my retirement plan and I don't know anything about investing. It seems like all my coworkers make more money with the funds they pick."

"If we end up taking over your retirement plan, I'd be happy to sit down with you one on one and give you an education," Frank offers.

Just then, Laura enters the reception area, and Frank introduces Rick to her. As they settle into Laura's office, she says, "I've been looking forward to this meeting—I don't think I've ever said that about shopping for my retirement plan before."

"Laura, before we dive in and discuss our ideas, let's talk about fiduciary responsibility," Rick says. "Frank mentioned that you're concerned about your fiduciary responsibilities and you don't have a handle on exactly what that means. Much like someone who's never had to have a cavity fixed before, your concerns boil down to fear of the unknown." Laura nods in agreement.

Rick continues, "The liability you've heard about essentially covers two areas. One: Make sure the plan is set up and functions in the best interest of its beneficiaries, which is you and your employees."

Laura interrupted, "Does that mean I can't cross-test and contribute more for me than for my employees?"

"No, you can still cross-test," Rick says.

"Then what does it mean to ensure the plan functions in the best interest of me and my employees?"

"It simply means that you need a defined process that describes why you chose a particular vendor, how you select the investment options available in the plan, and the ongoing process you use to monitor and evaluate the plan's investment options," Rick explains. "I would suggest you put into practice an investment policy statement."

Rick describes to Laura the process of writing and updating an investment policy statement. He shows her an example and explains how she would operate within the parameters set forth in that written document.

"Now, the second area of potential fiduciary liability is your employees' investment education," Rick continues. "Frank tells me you're not comfortable allowing your employees to select their funds and manage their own accounts."

Laura nods in agreement and says, "He's right, I wouldn't be comfortable with them managing my funds. Why should I be comfortable allowing them to manage their own accounts?"

"That's why we need to make sure your employees understand three basic concepts." Rick then outlines the key educational concepts that employees need to understand about employer-sponsored retirement plans.

Concept 1: Saving for retirement is important. Rick states that most people would never drive to a faraway destination without the aid of a map or instructions to get from point A to point B and without calculating how much gas money they'd need. "Yet people make the long journey from where they're at today to retirement without a road map," Rick points out. "They have no idea if they have enough money to achieve their retirement goals, to retire in the lifestyle they desire, or to ensure they don't outlive their retirement savings. As part of our service commitment, we'll help your employees understand how vital it is to save for retirement."

Concept 2: Tools and resources enable each person to calculate their retirement savings needs. Rick explains that they would provide worksheets, online tools, and one-on-one meetings with Frank to help Laura's employees determine how much they need to contribute to their retirement plans.

Concept 3: Frank can help employees set up a plan and properly diversify. Rick explains that Frank and his team will provide services to ensure that plan participants properly diversify their accounts to minimize the risk of large losses. Rick adds that, based on his brief chat with Laura's receptionist, she may be chasing performance. "Instead of building an asset allocation model to grow her savings, she's simply chasing yesterday's winners."

"Which are tomorrow's losers," Laura adds. "I understand all that. But I still don't understand where the liability comes from. Why are employees suing their employers?"

"Sometimes business owners select investment funds but don't take the time to ensure the funds continue to provide a respectable performance," Rick explains. "Employers are surprised to find themselves being sued because the investment lineup is substandard. Employees haven't been educated, aren't properly equipped to manage their accounts, and don't do a good job with their asset allocations. They try to hold their employers accountable for performing a duty they were never trained to do. Laura, you wouldn't let me go into your office and clean someone's teeth, would you?"

"Good heavens, no—not without proper training. I see your point."

"There are many different ways to incur fiduciary liability— and protect yourself against it." Rick gives Laura a primer on her fiduciary responsibilities. She becomes more comfortable with them, particularly after she hears that Frank will actively work with her to create an investment policy statement, set up appropriate files, and educate her employees.

"Now," she says, "how will you help me save a boatload of money every year?"

Rick chuckles. "Let's not get ahead of ourselves, Laura. We have an idea that may or may not apply to your situation. In the best-case scenario, we can take over your 401(k) plan and add a defined benefit plan."

"Oh, I should've guessed. But I'm not interested in a defined benefit plan," she states flatly.

"Why do you say that?" Rick asks.

"We used to have a defined benefit plan and it was expensive. I had to contribute the same amount of money for myself and every employee in my practice. The total contribution was more than my practice could afford. We discontinued that plan and started the 401(k) plan we have today."

"Frank tells me you have a cross-tested 401(k) profit-sharing plan and you like the flexibility of rewarding different groups or classifications of employees differently," Rick says.

"Yes, that's right. I like to reward my best employees a little more and, of course, reward myself the most," she adds, smiling.

"What if I told you that you could do that in a defined benefit plan?" Rick asks.

"What do you mean? I thought everyone had to receive the same amount. Isn't that the law?"

"What if I told you we could create a defined benefit plan that gives you the flexibility to have different benefit levels and even exclude some of your employees from the plan?"

"Interesting . . ." she says, although she still has a doubting look.

"Laura, with your permission, I'd like to ask you a question . . . you don't have to answer. When you decided to terminate the defined benefit plan and go with the 401(k) plan, were you trying to save one hundred and fifty thousand dollars a year?"

"Heavens, no. I could barely make ends meet in those days. I'd just bought this practice and was just starting out. Plus, to tell you the truth, I was into expensive new cars instead of saving for retirement. Now, driving a new car isn't important to me—preparing for my retirement is a lot more urgent."

"Exactly," Rick says. "You're at a different stage of your life now. You have the cash flow to support saving more than one hundred thousand dollars pretax, right?"

"Yes."

"Laura, do you have a Roth IRA?"

"No, because Frank tells me I make too much money to have one."

"Would you like to have one?"

"Yes. Who wouldn't like to put some money aside that would grow tax free?"

"Laura, what if I told you we could give you the same cross-tested 401(k) you have today and a defined benefits plan that would allow you to save substantially more money, plus allow you to save some of that money on an after-tax basis that would grow tax free?"

"That would be great," Laura replies. "Do you think I can save as much as one hundred and fifty thousand dollars a year?"

"Laura, if I can put a plan together that allows you to set aside that amount each year, how much would you be willing to pay for it?" Rick asks.

"I'm not going to tell you that, Rick. You tell me. What would that plan cost me?"

"How much do you think you'd save in taxes with that plan?"

Laura thinks for a moment and says, "Easily fifty thousand dollars a year in taxes."

"If I provided this plan design to you for ten thousand dollars, would you say, 'I'm ready to sign on the bottom line'?"

"You bet!"

"Great," Rick says. "To take the next step, we need you to provide us with a census of you and your employees. We'll use this information to run a series of illustrations to show you how much you could save and what the cost of that savings would be."

"I have a census right in here a file. Does this give you everything you need?" Laura asks.

Rick reviews the census and notes that it provides every employee's name, salary, sex, date of birth, and date of hire.

"Yes, this provides everything I need."

"Laura, who would you like to benefit the most? How would you like us to illustrate who gets what amount?" Rick asks.

"I'd like to clarify how much money I can save for myself and what my practice would have to contribute for each employee to make that happen."

The Dentist's Office: Part II

Two weeks later, Rick and Frank return to Laura's office. The three thoroughly review the illustrations showing different contribution levels, how much Laura could save every year, and the total amounts her dental practice would need to contribute to the plan for Laura and her employees. Laura is surprised and ecstatic to learn how much she could personally save while only making modest contributions to the profit-sharing plan for her employees.

"I took the liberty to calculate the total economic gain for you, including comparing tax savings versus administration costs," Rick says, handing her a piece of paper. Laura leans back in her chair as she considers all the figures. Finally, she looks up and smiles.

"Laura, do you feel the administrative cost is fair, given the benefit we would provide to you and your employees?"

"Yes, I'm comfortable with these fees," she says. "But remember, we talked about a Roth 401(k), too. Can I take advantage of saving after-tax money?"

Rick explains that Laura could defer up to $15,000 this year into a Roth 401(k), plus up to $5,000 a year in makeup contributions because she's over the age of 50. This money would be deferred on an after-tax basis and would grow tax free.

"Let me clarify one point. I can save most of my money as pretax dollars or set up part or all of it as after-tax Roth contributions?"

"You can do any combination of pretax and after-tax Roth savings as long as you don't exceed the 2006 federal limit for contributions—fifteen thousand dollars, plus the five thousand dollars a year in makeup contributions. Does that answer your question?"

"Yes."

"Do you have any more questions about these plans?"

"No, I think we've covered all my questions and concerns."

"Laura, would you have time to complete the paperwork this afternoon?" Rick asks.

"Yes, today's my office day, so my schedule is flexible. Let's do it!"

As Rick pulls out the application, Frank interrupts and asks, "Laura, don't you want to see the list of funds, test drive the Web site, or review the statements?"

Rick turns to Laura and says, "Laura, if you'd like, we can take the time to look through this list of funds. If you have any questions, please ask. This list has a wide variety of funds, and you'll recognize many of the names. If you'd like to go through this page by page, I'll be happy to take the extra time with you. Also, I can give you a tour of our Internet site and the statements—I'm sure you'll see that they're clear."

"No, Rick, I'm sure your funds are as good as any other company's," Laura responds. "Frankly, I don't care what the statements and Web site look like, as long as you design a plan that saves me this much money. Let's go ahead and fill out the paperwork."

Frank and Rick Debrief

As they depart Laura's office, Frank turns to Rick and asks, "How did you just do that?"

"What do you mean?"

"You just sold Laura a significant retirement plan without even showing her what your company does."

"That's right, Frank," Rick replies. "That's because Laura doesn't care about what my company can or can't do. Laura had a problem, and we brought a solution for her problem. A few years ago, I went to a seminar and learned about Solutions Based Selling. I discovered that it doesn't come down to product, although product does carry some weight. Clients have problems. There's pain, and it's up to us to find an ointment and make that pain go away. Some, like Laura, want to be aggressive in their savings. Sometimes the pain is about fear, like her fiduciary concerns. We have to help them deal with whatever their pain may be. When our clients talk with us, they need to make an emotional decision as much as a logical decision. We're not doing our clients any justice by only selling product. When you get right down to it, Frank, this business isn't about fund performance, fees, or expenses. It's about people. It's about finding solutions to people's problems. We have to understand their needs and then support those needs." Rick chuckles and adds, "Do you see what I mean, grasshopper?"

"Yes," Frank replied. "I'll start using this approach with all my clients. Obviously, it works."

STEP 5: FOLLOWING UP AFTER THE SALE

"Hi, Frank," Rick says. "I'm just calling to see how you're doing."

"Hi, Rick. I've never been better."

"Terrific. How are those two retirement plans doing?"

"They're doing great. I've been meeting with the employees and working hard to give both companies great service. By the way, I took your advice. After one of the enrollment meetings at Bob's company, I asked him about the financial impact on him and his company if something ever happened to Suzanne. Bob said it would be a catastrophe. I asked if he had key person disability and life insurance coverage on Suzanne. Rick, my question really took him by surprise; he had never thought about that. So I ran some quotes on key person disability and life policies, and Bob bought them both."

"That's great!" Rick says.

"There's more good news," Frank adds. "I created an estate plan for Bob and his wife, which included a second-to-die policy inside an irrevocable life insurance trust. Plus, Suzanne has already moved her personal accounts over to me."

"That's terrific!"

"On top of all that," Frank continues, "I know I did Bob a huge favor by helping to protect him from an exposure he never recognized by providing the key person life insurance policies. The compensation I've received from this ancillary business has far exceeded my expectations—and even my commission on that retirement plan."

"Congratulations! Hey, how about Doctor Laura? How's it going with her?" Rick asks.

"She just hired a junior partner," Frank replies. "In five years, she'll start phasing out of her dental practice and phasing into retirement. I told Laura the story you had shared with me about the business owner who sold his business but only got part of the money because the buyer was killed in a car accident. Laura is taking out a buy/sell life insurance policy on her new junior partner."

Frank continues, "Rick, I've been meaning to tell you something. I might have been able to win Laura's business without your help, but I never would have put together the plan design you created for her. And I wouldn't have been able to address her fiduciary concerns. So, even though I might have been able to sell some kind of plan without you, I'm glad I didn't. My client received a much better plan design, and we earned her trust, which is opening more doors for me."

"Thanks, Frank, I'm glad to hear that."

"Hey, Rick, while I have you on the phone, can we set a time to talk next week? I'm prospecting a few more clients for retirement plans—one or two are looking pretty good. I expect to have you back in Colorado Springs very soon . . ."

1

GLOSSARY OF
RETIREMENT PRODUCTS

You probably sell individual retirement plans in your practice and may be familiar with many of these plans. Keep in mind that service providers offer multiple plan designs featuring multiple products for small- to mid-size businesses looking to sponsor retirement plans. Various plan designs may incorporate a mix of the following retirement arrangements:

- *Traditional IRA.* An eligible individual may contribute to his own program in deductible (or nondeductible) dollars that grow tax-deferred; distributions are required at age 70½ and after.
- *Roth IRA.* Eligible individuals may contribute nondeductible dollars to their own plan with the potential benefit of tax-free buildup of income; unlike a traditional IRA, distributions are not required at any age.
- *Individual 401(k).* Offers maximum contributions and flexibility to owner-only businesses, husband-and-wife businesses, and small businesses with no eligible rank-and-file employees.

- *Roth 401(k)*. Allows investors to designate certain 401(k) contributions as "after tax," enabling them to withdraw these same dollars (and possibly earnings) tax-free at retirement.
- *Safe-harbor 401(k)*. Designed for small to large employers who want to offer a salary reduction plan with a maximum number of design options; typically offered to companies with a large percentage of highly compensated employees and, therefore, may be attractive for employers with top-heavy plans with low participation rates.
- *Age-weighted 401(k)*. Suitable for businesses with older, higher-paid owners and younger employees, this feature may allow larger contributions for older employees.
- *New comparability 401(k)*. For businesses interested in rewarding certain categories of employees based on age, tenure, or other reasonable business criteria, this plan's features may provide for higher contributions to certain categories.
- *The Social Security integration 401(k)*. Designed for businesses with higher-paid owners who aren't necessarily older, allows larger contributions to employees with incomes in excess of the taxable wage base.
- *SEP-IRA (Simplified Employee Pension plan)*. Offers the maximum deductible contributions of profit-sharing and money purchase plans without the fiduciary responsibility, administrative costs, and annual maintenance responsibilities.
- *SIMPLE-IRA (Savings Incentive Match Plan to Employee-owned account)*. Offers a 401(k)-type plan with employee and employer contributions but without the formal plan document, fiduciary responsibilities, and administrative costs and time.
- *403(b) plan*. Provides certain not-for-profit organizations with a means for their employees to save on a tax-deferred basis; typical client organizations include public and private schools, hospitals, private colleges, religious organizations, and charitable institutions.
- *457 plan*. Provides employees of government entities and non-church-controlled tax-exempt organizations a means to save on a tax-deferred basis.

- *Profit-sharing plan.* The employers' contributions may be made on a discretionary basis and are generally made out of profits from the business. Employers who would be likely candidates for this plan include those that don't desire an annual commitment or may experience cash flow inconsistencies, new businesses that may not be financially stable, and employers who wish to motivate their employees by tying employer contributions to company profits.
- *Money purchase plan.* In this qualified defined contribution retirement plan, the employer has a fixed obligation to make contributions each year according to the plan's contribution formula specified by the employer in the plan documents.
- *412(i) plan.* Allows business-owner clients to make substantial tax-deductible contributions through their business while accumulating a significant amount of money for their retirement.
- *Solo defined benefit plan.* Enables small business and self-employed clients age 45 or older to maximize their retirement contributions and dramatically cut their taxes; by maximizing retirement savings and minimizing income tax, eligible clients can "catch up" on their retirement savings.
- *Nonqualified deferred compensation.* In this customized arrangement to help employers attract, recruit, and retain select management and/or highly compensated employees and to help employees supplement their retirement income, the employer makes an unsecured promise to pay benefits in the future at the occurrence of specified events (for example, retirement, disability, or death) to select key employees in exchange for service yet to be performed.

2

MODEL INVESTMENT POLICY STATEMENT

The investment policy statement—an important document for employer-sponsored retirement plans—offers clear written communication regarding the plan process and provides protection against potential fiduciary liability.

ERISA requires all employer-sponsored retirement plans to have a procedure in place to establish and carry out the funding policy of the plan that is consistent with the objectives of the plan. The investment policy statement is one way to fulfill this requirement.

This written document reflects the plan's specific goals and objectives and should outline four major objectives:

1. The intended purpose of the plan
2. Its long-range investment framework
3. An outline of the investment selection
4. A monitoring and replacement process and a clear definition of related investment duties and responsibilities

The employer's fiduciaries and the plan's advisors should carefully draft this document, thoroughly review it, and keep it up to date.

The following model investment policy statement was drafted by the Profit Sharing 401(k) Council of America, a national not-for-profit association of plan sponsors, and is used here by permission.

PART I. THE PLAN

The ABC Company sponsors the ABC Defined Contribution Plan (the Plan) for the benefit of its employees. It is intended to provide eligible employees with the long-term accumulation of retirement savings through a combination of employee and employer contributions to individual participant accounts and the earnings thereon.

The Plan is a qualified employee benefit plan intended to comply with all applicable federal laws and regulations, including the Internal Revenue Code of 1986, as amended, and the Employee Retirement Income Security Act of 1974 (ERISA), as amended. (Optional: the Plan is intended to comply with ERISA Section 404c, and the choice disclosure required by the regulations will be met.)

The Plan's participants and beneficiaries are expected to have different investment objectives, time horizons, and risk tolerances. To meet these varying investment needs, participants and beneficiaries will be able to direct their account balances among a range of investment options to construct diversified portfolios that reasonably span the risk/return spectrum. Participants and beneficiaries alone bear the risk of investment results from the options and assets mixes that they select.

PART II. THE PURPOSE OF THE INVESTMENT POLICY STATEMENT

This investment policy statement is intended to assist the Plan's fiduciaries by ensuring that they make investment-related decisions in a prudent manner. It outlines the underlying philosophies and processes for the selection, monitoring, and evaluation of the investment options and investment managers utilized by the Plan. Specifically, this Investment Policy Statement:

- Defines the Plan's investment objectives
- Defines the roles of those responsible for the Plan's investments
- Describes the criteria and procedures for selecting investment options and investment managers
- Establishes investment procedures, measurement standards, and monitoring procedures
- Describes ways to address investment options and investment managers that fail to satisfy established objectives
- Provides appropriate diversification within investment vehicles
- (Optional) Describes the Plan's approach to unrestricted investment options (mutual fund window and self-directed brokerage), company stock, and advice

This Investment Policy Statement will be reviewed at least annually, and, if appropriate, can be amended to reflect changes in the capital markets, plan participant objectives, or other factors relevant to the Plan.

PART III. INVESTMENT OBJECTIVES

The Plan's investment options will be selected to:

- Maximize return within reasonable and prudent levels of risk
- Provide returns comparable to returns for similar investment options
- Provide exposure to a wide range of investment opportunities in various asset classes
- Control administrative and management costs

PART IV. ROLES AND RESPONSIBILITIES

Those responsible for the management and administration of the Plan's investments include, but are not limited to:

The ABC Company, which is responsible for selecting the trustee(s), hiring the record keeper and/or investment advisory consultants, and appointing the members of the investment committee (if one exists). If there is not an investment committee, the ABC Company is also responsible for:

- Establishing and maintaining the Investment Policy Statement
- Selecting investment options
- Periodically evaluating the Plan's investment performance and recommending investment option changes
- Providing Plan participant investment education and communication

The Plan's trustee(s), which is responsible for holding and investing plan assets in accordance with the terms of the Trust Agreement.

The investment managers, which are responsible for making reasonable investment decisions consistent with the stated approach of the Plan, and reporting investment results on a regular basis as determined by the Plan fiduciaries.

The record keeper, which is responsible for maintaining and updating individual account balances as well as information regarding plan contributions, withdrawals, and distributions.

The investment committee (if there is one), which is responsible for:

- Establishing and maintaining the Investment Policy Statement
- Selecting investment options
- Periodically evaluating the Plan's investment performance and recommending investment option changes
- Providing Plan participant investment education and communication

PART V. SELECTION OF INVESTMENTS AND MANAGERS

The selection of investment options offered under the Plan is among the ABC Company/investment committee's most important responsibilities. Set forth below are the considerations and guidelines employed in fulfilling this fiduciary responsibility.

Investment Selection. The Plan intends to provide an appropriate range of investment options that will span the risk/return spectrum. Further, the Plan investment options will allow Plan participants to construct portfolios consistent with their unique individual circumstances, goals, time horizons, and tolerance for risk. Major asset classes to be offered will include:

(This is where the classes of investments to be included in the Plan are to be listed. The appropriate benchmark and peer group for each investment will be noted.)

After determining the asset classes to be used, ABC Company/ the investment committee must evaluate investment managers and choose managers to manage the specific investment options. Each investment manager must meet certain minimum criteria:

- It should be a bank, insurance company, or investment management company or an investment advisor under the Registered Investment Advisers Act of 1940.
- It should be operating in good standing with regulators and clients, with no material pending or concluded legal actions.
- It should provide detailed additional information on the history of the firm; its investment philosophy and approach; and its principals, clients, locations, fee schedules, and other relevant information.

Assuming the minimum criteria are met, the particular investment under consideration should meet the following standards for selection:

- Performance should be equal to or greater than the median return for an appropriate, style-specific benchmark and peer group over a specified time period.
- Specific risk and risk-adjusted return measures should be established and agreed to by ABC Company/the investment committee and be within a reasonable range relative to an appropriate, style-specific benchmark and peer group.
- It should demonstrate adherence to the stated investment objective.
- Fees should be competitive compared to similar investments.
- The investment manager should be able to provide all performance, holdings, and other relevant information in a timely fashion, with specified frequency.

PART VI. INVESTMENT MONITORING AND REPORTING

The ongoing monitoring of investments must be a regular and disciplined process. It is the mechanism for revisiting the investment option selection process and confirming that the criteria originally satisfied remain so and that an investment option continues to be a valid offering. While frequent change is neither expected nor desirable, the process of monitoring investment performance relative to specified guidelines is an ongoing process.

Monitoring should occur on a regular basis (e.g., quarterly) and utilize the same criteria that were the basis of the investment selection decision. It will include a formal review annually. Further, unusual, notable, or extraordinary events should be communicated by the investment manager immediately to ABC Company/the investment committee. Examples of such events include portfolio manager or team departure, violation of investment guidelines, material litigation against the firm, or material changes in firm ownership structure, or announcements thereof.

If overall satisfaction with the investment option is acceptable, no further action is required. If areas of dissatisfaction exist, the investment manager and ABC Company/the investment committee must take steps to remedy the deficiency. If over a reasonable period the manager is unable to resolve the issue, termination may result.

PART VII. MANAGER TERMINATION

An investment manager should be terminated when ABC Company/the investment committee has lost confidence in the manager's ability to:

- achieve performance and risk objectives;
- comply with investment guidelines;
- comply with reporting requirements; or
- maintain a stable organization and retain key relevant investment professionals.

There are no hard and fast rules for manager termination. However, if the investment manager has consistently failed to adhere to one or more of the above conditions, it is reasonable to presume a lack of adherence going forward. Failure to remedy the circumstances of unsatisfactory performance by the investment manager, within a reasonable time, shall be grounds for termination.

Any recommendation to terminate an investment manager will be treated on an individual basis and will not be made solely based on quantitative data. In addition to those above, other factors may include professional or client turnover or material change to investment processes. Considerable judgment must be exercised in the termination decision process.

A manager to be terminated shall be removed using one of the following approaches:

- Remove and replace (map assets) with an alternative manager
- Freeze the assets managed by the terminated manager and direct new assets to a replacement manager
- Phase out the manager over a specific time period

- Continue the manager but add a competing manager
- Remove the manager and do not provide a replacement manager
- Navigate the manager to a brokerage window (if available)

Replacement of a terminated manager would follow the criteria outlined in Part V, Selection of Investments and Managers.

PART VIII. PARTICIPANT EDUCATION AND COMMUNICATION

The Plan will communicate to employees that they control their own investments, permit investment changes at least quarterly, and provide effective educational materials allowing employees to make informed decisions.

PART IX. COORDINATION WITH THE PLAN DOCUMENT

Not withstanding the foregoing, if any term or condition of this investment policy conflicts with any term or condition in the Plan, the terms and conditions of the Plan shall control.

PART X. FURTHER GUIDELINES (OPTIONAL)

Mutual fund windows. In an effort to provide some (but not total) investment flexibility, a mutual fund window option is offered as a way of providing additional investment options to Plan participants. In developing and maintaining the Plan's mutual fund window, ABC Company/the investment committee will evaluate the window provider for reasonable cost, fund availability, competitive service capability, and participant satisfaction. There will be an annual review to confirm competitiveness.

Self-directed brokerage. In an effort to provide total investment flexibility, a self-directed brokerage option is offered in the Plan. The Plan's self-directed brokerage option allows participants to invest in any publicly traded security, including stocks, bonds, and mutual funds, with the following exceptions: short sales, options, futures, limited partnerships, currency trading, and trading on margin. In developing and maintaining the Plan's self-directed brokerage option, ABC Company/the investment committee will evaluate the self-directed option provider for reasonable cost, competitive service capability, and participant satisfaction. There will be an annual review to confirm competitiveness.

Company stock. ABC Company stock is offered as an investment option pursuant to the terms of the Plan. Plan fiduciaries will be responsible for managing the investment of Plan assets in company stock according to the Plan document. ABC Company/ the investment committee will monitor the performance of ABC Company stock but not for the purpose of recommending levels of company stock investment in the Plan or the elimination of company stock as a Plan investment, as they may have access to inside information.

Advice. As with any designation of a service provider to the Plan, the designation of a company or individual to provide investment advice to plan participants and beneficiaries is an exercise of discretionary authority and control with respect to management of the plan. Therefore, ABC Company/the investment committee will act prudently and solely in the interest of the plan participants and beneficiaries both in making such designation(s) and in continuing such designations(s).

At a minimum, the investment advice by the selected provider should be unbiased and be based on sound asset allocation theory and in-depth fund analysis. It should also be tailored to each participant's circumstances. Monitoring will occur on an annual basis and utilize the same criteria that were the basis of the investment advisor selection decision.

Copyright ©2001 by the Profit Sharing/401(k) Council of America

3

ERISA COMPLIANCE CHECKLIST

Listed here are several questions you can review with employers to help ensure they're in compliance with ERISA.

Have you provided a Summary Plan Description, with summaries of any material modifications of the plan to employees who are eligible to participate in the plan? Plan sponsors (employers) need to distribute this information to all employees at three points in time:

1. Within 90 days of their eligibility to participate in the plan
2. Any time there are any material modifications to the plan
3. At least every ten years

Do you maintain copies of plan documents for examination by participants and beneficiaries? Eligible employees and their beneficiaries must have the ability to review plan documents within a reasonable time frame. Many employers don't have plan documents sorted, filed, and organized properly. Encourage those you work with to do so immediately.

Has the plan submitted employee deferrals in a timely manner? Elective deferrals can't be loaned to the company, used to pay expenses, or held for more time than administratively necessary.

Were the investments selected using a documented process? If a plan permits employees to select asset allocations (self-direct their accounts), fiduciaries (the company representatives who are responsible for the day-to-day administration of the plan) must make sure employees can properly diversify their accounts to minimize the risk of large losses. The investment choices should permit participants to create a diversified portfolio.

Are the investments monitored on a periodic basis using specific criteria? On an ongoing basis (annually, at minimum) the investments should be evaluated to ensure that they meet risk and performance criteria pursuant to the investment policy statement. Performance alone is not adequate. Many investment committees use criteria with names such as Alpha, Beta, Sharpe Ratio, the Information Ratio, Standard Deviation, Style Drift, Attribution Analysis, and more.

Do the participants have access to the information and education they require to make informed decisions? Participants need education on the importance of saving for retirement as well as the tools and resources required to calculate their individual retirement savings needs. Education will give them the ability to properly diversify their accounts. Employers are wise to keep documentation demonstrating that sufficient education was provided.

Do the plan fiduciaries meet regularly and maintain proper notes and documentation? Plan fiduciaries should meet on a periodic basis (annually, at minimum) to review the plan's design, its investments, and participants' demographics and to review past/future educational efforts.

Is the plan covered by a fidelity bond? Every plan fiduciary, and anyone who may have administrative capacity, is required to be bonded. The amount of the bond can't be less than 10 percent of the plan's assets but doesn't need to be more than $500,000.

Does the plan sponsor adhere to the plan documents? Employers must follow the provisions as stated within their plan documents. For example, if the document states that an employee must be employed by the company for one year and work a minimum of 1,000 hours to meet eligibility, the employer cannot make an exception and give a new employee immediate eligibility as part of the new employee's hiring contract.

Does the plan maintain an investment policy statement? While an investment policy statement isn't required, Section 402(b)(1) of ERISA states that plans must "provide a procedure for establishing and carrying out a funding policy in a method consistent with the objectives of the plan."

4

SETTING UP A DUE DILIGENCE FILE

To help employers set up appropriate processes and monitor the plans themselves, we suggest working with the day-to-day administrators at your client companies to set up a proper due diligence file.

The umbrella due diligence file may contain the following files:

- *Plan document file.* Contains the plan documents, adoption agreements, the Summary Plan Description, and any plan amendments.
- *IRS determination file.* Contains copies of requests and responses to obtaining a letter of determination from the Internal Revenue Service.
- *SPDs file.* Contains copies of the Summary Plan Description for distribution.
- *Audit file.* Contains copies of prior year's audits and the SAS70 where applicable.
- *Testing file.* Create a new file for each year's nondiscrimination testing and compliance workup.
- *Annual reports file.* Contains a copy of the employer's annual reports.
- *Board of director resolutions file.* Contains any resolutions passed by the company's board of directors, including the original resolution to create the plan.
- *Fidelity/fiduciary bond file.* Contains copies of the actual policies.

- *Contract/service agreements file.* Contains a copy of any service agreements, trust agreements, insurance contracts, or professional contracts.
- *Meeting minutes file.* Contains detailed notes from any meetings related to the plan.
- *5500/schedules file.* Create a new file for each year's tax return and related schedules.
- *QDRO file.* Contains any qualified domestic relations orders that the plan processes.
- *Notifications file.* Contains a copy of all notifications distributed to the employees such as a Sarbanes-Oxley Notice, Safe Harbor Notice, 404(c) notices, etc.
- *Distributions file.* Contains a copy of any distributions.
- *Enrollment file.* Contains copies of all enrollment and beneficiary forms.
- *Investment committee file.* Contains information related to the selection of the committee members, the ongoing education provided to ensure they're qualified to carry out their jobs, copies of forms distributed to committee members that describe their responsibilities, meeting notes, etc.
- *Investments file.* Contains information pursuant to all investments made available under the plan.
- *Investment selection and monitoring file.* Contains information related to how the investments are selected and monitored on an ongoing basis and the criteria established to remove or add a fund.
- *Communication and education file.* Contains a history of education, including whether the education was provided through an employee meeting or mailing, a record of who provided the information, the type of education provided, samples of the documents participants received, and which participants received the education.
- *Communications file.* Contains communications between the plan sponsor and the investment professional servicing the account.

Being familiar with these terms and requirements will help you create solid relationships with your clients—relationships built on trust and confidence. Remember, you don't need a law degree to support your clients' fiduciary needs. Your service provider—your partner in your retirement plans business—will assist in educating you and your clients to meet their fiduciary responsibilities and alleviate this potential source of stress.

OPPORTUNITY DIAGNOSTIC WORKSHEET

Opportunity Diagnostic Worksheet

1) Opportunity Qualification (0 to 17 Points)	Point Value
Measurement Criteria:	
☐ The plan sponsor is open to making a change.	
☐ We know when they will review their 401k plan.	
☐ Hartford Life is already providing product/services to the business.	
☐ We have access to the senior decision maker to make a presentation.	
Total Score:	

2) Competitive Situation (-5 to 5 Points)	Point Value
Measurement Criteria:	
☐ A competitive broker (or vendor) has a small share of the customer's business.	
☐ A competitive broker (or vendor) has their own supporters in the account.	
☐ We fully understand the competitive broker's (or vendor's) selling strategy.	
☐ We have developed a plan to secure this account.	
Total Score:	

3) Customer Knowledge (0 to 13 Points)	Point Value
Measurement Criteria:	
☐ We understand the department(s) within the company that our solution impacts. For example, we know the department's objectives, strategies, key projects, and challenges.	
☐ We know the customer's principle line of business.	
☐ We know their target market, their competition, and how they differentiate themselves from their competitors.	
☐ We know their key objectives and the strategies they will implement to achieve these objectives.	
☐ We know the challenges facing them in their marketplace.	
☐ We know key business issues from your/our discussions with your contacts.	
Total Score:	

4) Strength of Support (0 to 35 Points)	Point Value
Measurement Criteria:	
☐ We have identified one or more key players in the company to align with.	
☐ We have access to contacts who are open to sharing information.	
☐ We have built relationships with contacts who will give us information they wouldn't give the competitor.	
☐ We have contacts who believe our product or service is superior to the competition's and are willing to assist us (i.e., a champion).	
☐ We have a contact who wants you to win because of their strong relationship with you.	
☐ We have more than one supporter/champion/coach.	
Total Score:	

5) Impact of Detractors (-25 to 0 Points)	Point Value
Measurement Criteria:	
☐ We have identified a contact in the account that is aligned with a competitive broker (or vendor).	
☐ We have contacts who have verbalized their belief that the competitor's product is superior.	
☐ We have contacts who want us to lose and are blocking our selling strategy.	
☐ Your contact forces us to work through them and restricts access to other people.	
Total Score:	

6) Decision-Making Process (0 to 27 Points)	Point Value
Measurement Criteria:	
☐ We know who made the previous decision.	
☐ We know who will have influence on the decision.	
☐ We know who truly owns the decision.	
☐ We know the difference between who will be "making the recommendation" versus who will be making the decision.	
Total Score:	

Summary	Score
1) Opportunity Qualification (0 to 17 Points)	
2) Competitive Situation (-5 to 5 Points)	
3) Customer Knowledge (0 to 13 Points)	
4) Strength of Support (0 to 35 Points)	
5) Impact of Detractor (-25 to 0 Points)	
6) Decision-Making Process (0 to 27 Points)	
Total:	

E. Thomas Foster Jr., Esq., is The Hartford's national spokesperson for employer retirement plans. An ERISA attorney, Foster works directly with broker/dealer firms to promote the sale of 401(k) programs and other qualified retirement plan products, as well as to enhance The Hartford's brand identity for group retirement products. He also works closely with financial professionals to help them build their retirement plan businesses.

Foster has nearly 30 years of defined contribution retirement plan experience that spans product development, training, marketing, and relationship management with wholesalers and broker/dealer firms. He is an acknowledged industry expert in retirement plan legislation, regulation, and compliance testing.

Prior to joining The Hartford, Foster supported John Hancock's institutional sales and marketing department as well as John Hancock's broker/dealer community. Before that, he was assistant vice president of Aetna Life Insurance and Annuity Company. He also founded Foster Financial, a consulting firm specializing in employee benefit plans.

Foster has obtained membership in the following groups: Massachusetts Bar Association, Boston Bar Association, American Bar Association, the American Trial Lawyers Association, and the United States Supreme Court Bar. He has conducted lectures for trade organizations, including the following: U.S. League of Savings International, American Institute of Banking, National Association of Mutual Savings Banks, Credit Union Leagues and State Savings Leagues (in 44 states), Life Office Management Association (LOMA), Society of Pension Administrators and Record Keepers (SPARK), and Phoenix-Hecht. He has also conducted a series of accredited legal, certified public accounting, and financial planning seminars in 48 states.

Foster has appeared on Bloomberg Radio, CNN Radio (Houston), TheStreet.com, Sirius Satellite Radio, and WTNM (Memphis). He has been quoted and/or published in the following: 410(k)wire.com, *Advisor Today, American Banker, Barron's, Business Finance Magazine, CFO Magazine,*

Dallas Morning News, Defined Contribution News, Denver Post, Dow Jones News Service, *Employee Benefit News, Financial Planning, Financial World,* Gannett News Service, *Income Planning Online, Institutional Investor, Investment News, Investors Business Daily, Kansas City Star, Kiplinger's Personal Finance,* the *Lexington Herald Leader, Los Angeles Business Journal, Los Angeles Times, Money Management Executive, Money Management Letter, Morristown Daily Record, Mutual Fund Magazine, National Underwriter, Pension and Investments, Pension World, Plan Sponsor, Smart Money,* and the *Wall Street Journal.*

Todd D. Thompson is vice president, North Central Division, for The Hartford's Retirement Plans Group.

In this position, he is responsible for sales and marketing of corporate retirement plans through key accounts as well as developing marketing materials and seminars for use by the national sales force. Thompson also serves as spokesperson for The Hartford's retirement plans at national and regional meetings for financial broker/dealer firms, industry associations, and corporate meetings.

Thompson has earned many awards for his military and community involvement as well as his professional successes. He was awarded the Junior Chamber of Commerce Outstanding Regional Involvement Award, The Hartford Sales Leader of the Year Award, and The Hartford Sales Professional of the Year Award. Since 1996, he has served on the NASD Board of Arbitration. Thompson is also a member of the National Military Intelligence Association and the United States Naval Institute.

Share the message!

Bulk discounts
Discounts start at only 10 copies and range from 30% to 55% off retail price based on quantity.

Custom publishing
Private label a cover with your organization's name and logo. Or, tailor information to your needs with a custom pamphlet that highlights specific chapters.

Ancillaries
Workshop outlines, videos, and other products are available on select titles.

Dynamic speakers
Engaging authors are available to share their expertise and insight at your event.

Call Kaplan Publishing Corporate Sales at 1-800-621-9621, ext. 4444, or e-mail kaplanpubsales@kaplan.com

KAPLAN)

PUBLISHING